What is economics about?

Economics arises from the need to choose how to spend what we have, to apportion our resources – to economize, in fact.

Would you rather go on holiday or buy a new sofa? Would you prefer your government to spend more on education or reduce taxes? Should healthcare be free?

Questions like this lie at the heart of economics. They require us to choose how to use the financial resources available to us or our government, knowing that choosing one thing often means giving up another. They arise when we have to deal with scarcity – with choosing how to allocate limited resources.

These questions come about because for most people – and all governments – money is a limited resource. You might not have enough money to buy both a sofa and a holiday. A government might not have enough money to improve education and reduce taxes. It is not only about money; land and time are also limited resources.

If there were plenty of everything – unlimited food, land, housing, healthcare, education, transport, books – there would be no need for money, no need to choose or prioritize one thing over another, and consequently no need for economics.

Never enough

All the things we use – the food, housing and books – are called resources by economists. Most of them are in limited supply; they are, in economics-speak, scarce resources. Economists use 'scarce' in a slightly different way from everyone else. They don't mean the resource is rare or in short supply in the way that snow leopards are scarce. They mean simply that the supply of the resource is limited: either it is not renewable, or it is not renewable at the rate at which it is used. So oil is a scarce resource, even though in some countries there is plenty of it, because eventually it will run out and cannot be replenished. Economics is, essentially, the process of making choices about how to use scarce resources.

A very few things are essentially unlimited in their supply. Examples are air, sea-water, sunlight and wind power. Economists generally call these free goods, though in reality there is a limit to air and sea-water.

How to choose

Scarcity forces us to make choices. We might choose whether to use our time maintaining a vegetable garden or playing a sport; we have limited time and have to choose how best to use it. A business might choose to use its limited number of staff to make wheelbarrows or ladders, according to which it thinks will be more profitable. A government might choose whether to spend more on welfare payments or on road-building.

In each case, we have to weigh up the costs and benefits. There is often a trade-off: this generally means that having one thing requires us to relinquish another. If you spend your money on a holiday, you may not have enough to spend on new furniture. If you work part-time in order to spend more time with your family, you will earn less money than if you work full-time. You can choose to have (or give up) either money or free time.

Lost and costly opportunities

Economists apply mathematics to these commonplace ideas, making it possible to create useful models to explain what happens in an economy and help individuals, businesses and governments make plans for the future.

Imagine a farmer who can grow both strawberries and raspberries on her land. She only has a limited amount of land, so must decide the most profitable way of using it.

If the farmer chooses to grow more strawberries, she must grow fewer raspberries, and vice versa. If we draw a graph, we can calculate the opportunity cost of growing each type of fruit. The farmer has three polytunnels, so must choose how many to allocate to strawberries and how many to raspberries.

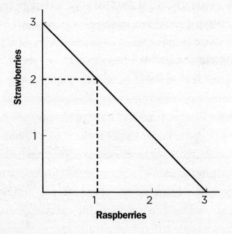

If the farmer decides to use two polytunnels for strawberries, she then has only one polytunnel in which to grow raspberries. For each polytunnel of strawberries she grows, the opportunity cost is one polytunnel of raspberries, and for

NO LIMITS

Free goods can be produced with no cost in terms of resources. Ironically, this leads to a definition of free goods that can include or exclude identical items. Intangible goods such as a computer program, web page or ebook, which can be downloaded any number of times without using more resources, are free goods. The original composition, though, has taken resources to create (in the form of time, skill and effort). If a publisher makes a charge for the program or ebook, identical copies of the item are no longer a free good because the consumer has to use resources (money) to acquire them. Intellectual property rights convert a free good to a scarce good in recognition of the resources used in its original creation.

A POST-SCARCITY ECONOMY

Some futurists have suggested that nanotechnology (creating things at a molecular level) might one day be used to convert any type of matter into any other matter of the same mass. All goods would then become free goods as they would be limitlessly interchangeable – there would be no restriction on any particular type of good.

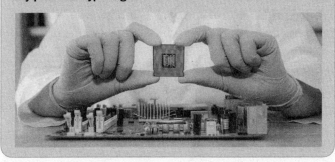

each polytunnel of raspberries, the opportunity cost is one polytunnel of strawberries (see graph on facing page).

The curve gets curvy

In this case, the opportunity-cost graph is a straight line: each polytunnel of strawberries costs one polytunnel of raspberries and vice versa. But it is rarely this straightforward.

Here's another example: suppose we have an island that has rich, fertile land on one side and rocky scrubland on the other. The principal farming products of the island are goats and wheat. The islanders have to decide how to allocate the land. This time, the opportunity cost is not a straight line because the resource (the land) is uneven. It will be very difficult to grow wheat on the rocky scrubland – little will take root there. But goats can tolerate scrubland. It is also easy to keep goats on the fertile land, but that would be a waste because it is good for growing wheat.

The islanders begin by growing wheat on the fertile land. As they run out of fertile land, the yield of wheat per acre will drop. On the rocky scrubland, the yield is low. This means the opportunity cost involved in growing wheat rises, as the islanders are forced to use less suitable land. They might need to displace one goat per 400 kg of wheat on the fertile land, but displace four goats to gain 400 kg of wheat on the scrubland. The opportunity cost of 400 kg of wheat therefore varies between one and four goats.

Conversely, the opportunity cost of keeping a goat on the fertile land is 400 kg of wheat, but the opportunity cost of keeping a goat on the scrubland is only 400 ÷ 4 = 100 kg of wheat.

OPPORTUNITY COST

Economists call this trade-off 'opportunity cost'. The opportunity cost of a new sofa is the holiday you can't afford; and the opportunity cost of spending hours playing sport is the vegetable garden you won't have time to maintain.

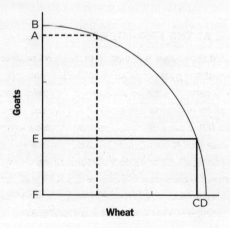

The graph on page 12 shows that the opportunity cost in goats of the first crop of wheat is low, just AB. As we move further along the curve, using ever more unsuitable land for growing wheat, the opportunity cost rises. The small yield of wheat represented by CD comes at the cost of a lot of potential goats (EF). The largest total production (of goats and wheat together) comes somewhere in the middle of the curve. This represents the point at which the best land is used to produce wheat and the worst land is used to produce goats. It is the most productive use of resources. At this point, the economy is as successful as it can be in this scenario.

More and less: supply and demand

On page 10, the simple graph of the fruit farmer's opportunity cost in growing strawberries and raspberries indicates no way of choosing which crop to grow; the choice is up to the farmer. But there are other factors to consider. If she produces just one crop, perhaps not enough people will want to buy it. In economic terms, this means she must decide whether there will be sufficient demand for (say) raspberries to ensure that the entire supply is sold. If demand is low, she will have to

WORKING AT THE FRONTIERS

The curve that shows how a country can divide its resources between wheat and goats is called a production possibility frontier (PPF) curve. If a nation produces at any point along the curve then all its resources are in use. If it produces inside the curve (to the left of the line), it has unused resources and is less productive than it could be. It can only produce at a point outside (to the right) of the curve if circumstances change. Perhaps farmers should start planting wheat with a higher yield or a variety that tolerates poorer quality soil, or maybe they should increase plot yield by applying more fertilizer.

Basic needs vary from country to country: warm clothing is a basic need of people living in Scandinavian countries.

sell raspberries for a lower price to get rid of them. Otherwise there's a danger she won't sell them before they rot. She might decide it is safer and more profitable to split her resources (polytunnels, fertilizer, farmworkers) between two crops. It increases the likelihood of selling all her produce, and even charging a higher price for it if demand is high compared with the supply. Supply and demand are central to shaping an economy (see Chapter 3).

Wants and needs

Consumers, those who buy or 'consume' goods and services, use their resources to obtain the things they need and want. As long as they have enough money to buy everything they need, they can use what is left over to buy the things they want. In economics, the distinction between needs and wants is important.

Needs must be met in order for a person to survive. They include food, drink, shelter and sufficient clothes to keep us warm. These are our most basic needs. Other needs vary according to time and place. For example, people living in Scandinavia need lots of warm clothes, whereas people living in Niger do not. Items considered necessary vary between cultures, and change over time. In the modern world, a car could be considered a necessity in rural areas because of the difficulty of getting around without one. In the past, a horse was a necessity, but now it is a luxury. Economists assess and decide what people in different circumstances need in order to have an acceptable standard of living.

Once basic needs have been met, any surplus money can be spent meeting wants. Unlike needs, wants are limitless. We need a certain amount of food and sufficient shelter and clothing to protect us from the weather, but our wants go on and on. Once we have enough food, we might want tastier food. We might want a larger house, a better car, more holidays – there is no end to what people want. All but the very wealthiest have to decide how to allocate their money. And even the wealthiest have to choose how to spend their time, as we all have a limited lifespan.

In Niger, basic needs include food, water, shelter and healthcare provision.

For the farmer who grows raspberries and strawberries, it's necessary to make the fruit appealing because consumers don't *need* it. (Although they need food, they don't necessarily need these particular types of food.) People might choose to spend money on these rather than on other luxury food items, such as ice cream, or on other fruit, such as apples. One thing that determines how consumers spend their money is price.

In the market

When economists use the term market, they mean anywhere, real or virtual, where buyers and sellers interact to exchange goods and services for money. They talk about 'markets' for different goods and services. There is, for example, a market for electricity and a market for motorbikes. There are usually many sellers and many buyers. The sellers try to attract buyers, competing with other sellers in the same market by offering more attractive prices, better quality products, and so on. There is also competition between markets, especially in the case of goods that satisfy wants rather than needs.

The stock market is just one example of an environment where buyers and sellers compete to sell their merchandise.

How to make an economy

An economy only emerges when there are people who interact to produce and exchange goods and services. There are economies of all sizes, from our own household economy to the wider local economy, which is part of a national economy. The national economy is part of a global economy.

If we lived isolated lives, growing all the food we ate, making our own clothes, building our own homes, caring for and educating our own children and dealing with our own healthcare problems, there would be no economic activity. With an economy, markets grow up for different goods and services, a means of exchange emerges (today this is money, but once it was barter – see Chapter 1), and a need to allocate resources arises.

Economics deals with how people – individuals, societies and nations – allocate resources in order to produce the goods and services required to meet people's wants and needs. An economy faces three important questions:

- **What** will be produced? There are limited resources, so they have to be allocated with care.

> *'The only function of economic forecasting is to make astrology look respectable.'*
>
> Ezra Solomon, Professor of Economics, Stanford University (1985)

- **How** will production be organized? There are different ways of making goods and delivering services. An economy will seek the most efficient methods of production to make the most of its resources.
- **Who** will benefit from the goods and services produced? Some goods and services will be for public use and others will be for private use. The distribution of wealth in a society is related to this question.

The limits of economics

Economics is not a science, like physics, in which new theories can be proved or disproved through experimentation. Many of the issues touched on in this book remain open for discussion, and different economists often have opposing views about how they should be tackled or interpreted. Even when dealing with the most pressing economic questions, such as how to save a failing national economy or combat famine in sub-Saharan Africa, economists wrangle over competing ideas and theories. Economics is a relatively new discipline and economies evolve and change rapidly. Economists haven't got it all right yet, by a long way.

CHAPTER 1

What is money anyway?

Trade, or commerce, is a fundamental part of economics, and money is at its heart. So what does money really represent?

Money is any token, physical or virtual, that can be used in trade. It might have intrinsic value, such as a disc of gold, or it might have only a symbolic value, like a printed slip of paper with a fancy design. It might have no physical existence, like the virtual currency bitcoin – a digital currency that operates independently of the main banking system. Of course, even the 'intrinsic' value of a gold coin is culturally determined. Gold is of limited use outside jewellery and commerce. It is now used in electronics, but that use emerged long after gold was first considered valuable. It's easier to make crowns and jewellery from gold than other metals because it's soft and non-corrosive – but you could say the same of plastic. Crowns and jewellery are not essential to survival – they are not 'needs'.

Bartering doesn't go well

Try to imagine a world in which there is no form of money. If you want something that you can't find or make yourself, you need to persuade someone who has it to give it to you. They will probably be unwilling to give it for free, but might swap it for something you have. This is called bartering. If you have a mammoth skin and want some watermelons, it might take a long time to find someone with watermelons who wants a mammoth skin. If the person with watermelons wants a clay bowl, you might have to trade a mammoth skin for a clay bowl, then trade the bowl for watermelons (if you can find someone with watermelons who wants a clay bowl). You can see how bartering quickly becomes a complex, time-consuming and often frustrating endeavour. This problem, called the coincidence of wants, or double coincidence of wants, makes such systems unwieldy and inefficient.

Instead, most societies have developed some form of exchange mechanism. This works on the basis that everyone agrees some token (cowrie shells, perhaps) represents value.

GOLDEN CHAINS

The 16th-century philosopher Sir Thomas More satirized humankind's greed for gold in his book *Utopia*. More's Utopians see gold as corrupting, so put it to unglamorous use: 'Their chamber-pots and close-stools are made of gold and silver. . . . Of the same metals they also make chains and fetters for their slaves; on some of whom, as a badge of infamy, they hang an ear-ring of gold, and make others wear a chain or a coronet of the same metal. And thus they take care, by all possible means, to render gold and silver of no esteem. Hence it is that, while other countries part with these metals as though one tore out their bowels, the Utopians would look upon giving-in all they had of them, when occasion required, as parting only with a trifle, or as we should esteem the loss of a penny.

'They find pearls on their coast, and diamonds and carbuncles on their rocks. They seek them not, but if they find them by chance, they polish them and give them to their children for ornaments, who delight in them during their childhood. But when they come to years of discretion, and see that none but children use such baubles, they lay them aside of their own accord; and would be as much ashamed to use them afterward, as grown children among us would be of their toys.'

Sir Thomas More, *Utopia*, Book 2 (1516)

The value can be transferred between people and exchanged for goods and services. This makes it easy to trade a mammoth skin for cowrie shells then take the shells to someone who has watermelons. The watermelon farmer can use the shells to buy a chair or a boat or a chicken – whatever he or she needs. As everyone in the community accepts that cowrie shells have value, they become a means of exchange – or money.

The four functions of money

In 1875, British economist William Jevons set out the four functions of money in his book *Money and the Mechanism of Exchange*. Money, he said, is a medium of exchange, a common measure of value, a standard of value and a store of value. Some economists have argued that storing money means you can't spend (exchange) it, and spending it means you can't save (store) it, so the two are mutually exclusive. But money can serve both functions at different times.

A modern approach often lists three functions for money:

- a medium of exchange
- a store of value
- a unit of account

It is called a medium of exchange as it facilitates the exchange (swapping) of goods and services, acting as an intermediary between disparate items such as mammoth skins and watermelons. As a store of value, it's important that whatever is chosen as the means of exchange does not readily deteriorate or decay. This is one reason for choosing gold. It would not be sensible to choose, say, fresh fruit as a medium of exchange because it would soon rot.

Economists recognize two types of value: the utility (usefulness) of a particular good or service, and the power of a good or service when exchanged to acquire other goods and services. Anything used as money has exchange value. It can also have utility value, as we shall see.

The last function, a unit of account, means there must be a consistent way of measuring or counting money and that it provides the unit for pricing other items. This is served by currency: we count money in dollars, pounds, euro, yuan, yen, pesos and so on.

WHEN MONEY GOES WRONG

When an economy fails, prices may rise beyond all sensible measure and each unit of currency will then buy less and less – its exchange value falls. In this case, money itself is no longer a good store of value. The classic example of this is the period in the 1920s when the German currency, the mark, became virtually worthless. Something that cost one mark in 1918 cost three billion marks in 1923. As a result, some people in Germany began to use other currencies or media of exchange in preference to the mark (see Chapter 14).

Commodity money

Physical items used as money are called commodity money. The item itself must have recognized intrinsic value. Items that have been used as commodity money include:

- Buckskins and beaver pelts in North America. Hudson Bay had an official exchange rate for beaver pelts. One beaver pelt could be exchanged for two pairs of scissors, five pounds of sugar, 20 fish-hooks or a pair of shoes. Twelve beaver pelts would buy you a gun.
- Decorative items such as shells, mirrors, beads and decorated belts. Part of the payment that Dutch traders made to Native Americans when they bought Manhattan Island in 1626 was in beads.

- Food items which are slow to perish, such as salt, peppercorns, barley, rice, dried fish and cattle.
- Tobacco and cigarettes. Cigarettes have often been used by soldiers and prisoners as currency. A full economy based on cigarettes grew up in some prisoner-of-war camps in World War II.

THE ISLAND OF STONE MONEY

On the Pacific island of Yap, wheel-shaped stones have been used as money for centuries. Some are small, but others very large – up to 3.6m (12 ft) across and weighing over 4,000 kg (4 tons). Made of limestone mined and carved in Palau, they were moved by bamboo canoe to Yap.

The agreed value of a stone depends on its size, craftsmanship and history. The most valuable stones, paradoxically, are those that killed no one in transit and those that killed most people in transit. The largest stones are rarely moved; trade consists only of recording a change in ownership. One stone even fell into the sea during transport to Yap and was still traded because access to it was not important. Everyone knew where it was and who owned it. Ownership of a stone that can't be retrieved from the ocean is an early example of virtual money.

THREE HEADS FOR THAT DRAGON JAR

Some of the Penan people in Borneo used the severed heads of their enemies as tributes to the spirits that had power over rice. Heads were offered to make the rice grow, but also became an item of value in their own right, because of their efficacy as spirit-bribes. There was no physical trade in heads, though, as trading them was considered unlucky. Instead, a head was equivalent to a living slave or captive, which could be traded. Some items had a value as 'virtual heads'. A dragon jar – a large receptacle with a green glaze and dragon motif, imported from China – was valued at three heads. If someone killed a person, requiring a tribute to the bereaved family of three heads, the debt could be discharged by the transfer of a dragon jar.

Modern money

For most of us, money is counted in units of a specific currency – dollars, pounds, euros, yen, yuan, lire, dinar and so on. This is called fiat money – the items exchanged have no intrinsic value, but they are agreed to have value for the sake of running the economy.

We are used to fiat money in the form of coins and notes, but increasingly also in virtual form. In the developed world today, people are less likely to be paid in cash. Their salary is usually deposited in their bank as a figure that increases their balance, and is often spent by using a card that authorizes a business to reduce the balance, or by setting up a direct debit or standing order that lets creditors take away some of the balance on a regular basis. We might sometimes withdraw some cash – but for most of us today cash is not really the dominant form of money (see Chapter 17).

Increasingly, money has become dissociated from the real, physical world. Money is now largely theoretical and there is nowhere near as much cash in existence as there is 'money' in the economic system. The money that is held only as electronic records is called bank money, for fairly obvious reasons.

Bank money is used to move money between financial institutions, governments, large corporations and so on. If you pay $20 to a bookshop using a debit card, there is no physical movement of actual money between your bank and the bookshop's bank. The entire transaction, and all similar transactions, are carried out using bank money.

A run on the bank

In the film *Mary Poppins*, Michael, the young son of Mr Banks, is reluctant to deposit his money in a bank. Michael demands his tuppence (two old pennies, or 2d) back, when the bank manager snatches it from him. Other customers who witness the scene misunderstand what is happening, and assume the bank can't honour a young customer's demand for tuppence. A 'run' on the bank ensues – that is, everyone tries to withdraw their money at the same time. This, in a nutshell, is what causes a run on a bank: too many depositors want their money back at once, and the bank can't honour all its debts immediately. A run generally starts because of a loss

of confidence in the bank, and then becomes a self-fulfilling prophecy. In fact, if at any point all customers tried to take all their money out of the banks, the banks would not be able to honour the deposits. Usually only a minority of people want their money at any one time and everyone else believes they can access it if they need to. In this way, the illusion and the banking system are sustained.

Genuine bank runs are relatively rare. In 1872, in Canada, there was a run on the Montreal City and District Savings Bank; and there were bank runs in the USA during the Great Depression of the 1930s. There were bank runs of a slightly different type on Northern Rock in the UK in 2007, Landsbanki, one of the largest banks in Iceland, in 2008, and the Greek banks in 2015.

How much money is there?

To put it simply, bank money exists provided people believe in it. If we all stopped believing in it and instead wanted it in hard cash, the system would collapse because bank money isn't really there (depending on your definition of 'really').

ASSETS AND LIABILITIES

An asset is anything that can be owned and which produces value (money). Assets include houses, money in the bank, a promise from someone to pay you money, or a machine for making something.

A liability is the opposite of an asset. A liability is something that entails a cost or obligation to pay for something in money or by some other means. Liabilities include an outstanding mortgage on a house, or a promise to buy a present for someone or deliver a lecture for free.

Assets and liabilities are always equally matched: your mortgage liability is equivalent to the bank's asset – a claim on part of the value of your house. If you owe $200,000 (a liability), the bank has an asset of $200,000 of value in the house.

There are different ways of talking about how much money there is and therefore about what constitutes 'really'. In the USA, the two most important measures of the money supply are M0 and M1. Other countries use similar measures, sometimes with additional categories.

- M0 is the total stock of cash – coins and notes – held by individuals and in banks and bank reserves. There is about $5 trillion (£3.25 trillion) of M0 in the world.
- M1 includes M0 and assets that are easily converted into cash (such as bank deposits in 24-hour access accounts). M1 comes to around $25 trillion (£16.25 trillion).
- M2 includes M0 and M1 and longer-term, less liquid assets such as money tied up in savings accounts. It comes to around $60 trillion (£39 trillion).

CHAPTER 2

What goes into making things?

Long ago, there were no manufactured goods. Now, almost everything is processed in some way.

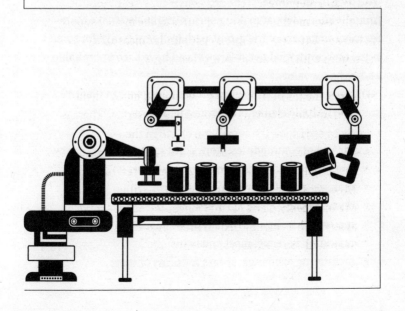

Our distant ancestors wandered the plains picking berries and roots and hunting animals that moved slowly enough to be killed easily. At some point, they realized that sharpened stones and sticks could make catching animals easier, and making a fire to cook them made them tastier. The person who invested time in sharpening a stone and fashioning a spear was making an early form of economic decision: at the cost of time and labour (his or her own) and using a free resource (a stone and a stick), he or she made a manufactured good. The opportunity cost in making the spear was the time that could have been spent doing something else.

The utility of the spear (the benefit of the spear to the individual) was greater than the utility of the stone, stick and labour to make it, as it would secure food more easily and save time in the future. So making the spear added value: that is the defining feature of manufacturing industry.

Starting in business

An individual adept at making spears might also make them for other members of the group, perhaps in exchange for some skins to wear or food to eat. A spear can have both *utility* value and *exchange* value.

In this example of early entrepreneurship, we can identify some of the basic elements of economic activity:

- the use of commodities: stones and sticks
- employing labour: the spear-maker's effort
- making manufactured goods: spears
- representing capital: spears
- increasing utility: the benefit of a spear
- providing revenue: meat and skins
- facilitating exchange: spears for skins or meat.

Factors of production

Economists talk of the factors of production, which go into producing any manufactured goods. Neoclassical economics considers there to be three factors of production: land, capital and labour.

Land not only covers the land itself but also anything on it, above it or drawn from it. This means that natural resources such as trees growing on the land and oil underground also count as land. For the spear-maker, sticks and stones come from land.

Capital is everything that can be used in the production of goods to gain more goods. Capital goods are not used up in the manufacture of more items (though they might eventually wear out). In the modern world, capital includes large items such as factory premises, machinery and vehicles (lorries and tractors, say), and small items such as a gardener's tools and an artist's paintbrushes. For our early ancestor, the completed spear is a capital good, as it is used to secure food.

Labour is the work that people put in to make something. If you make something for yourself, your own effort is the labour involved. When people work for an employer they sell their labour in exchange for wages. (Economists refer to 'wages' even when pay is a monthly salary or a one-off fee.) The early spear-maker uses his or her own labour.

Defining capital

The traditional, narrow definition of capital – objects that are not used up in the production of goods – has been superseded in more recent economic thinking. Intangible forms of capital are now included, such as the skills of an individual trained to carry out a particular job, or the goodwill built up by a company through its dealings with customers and suppliers:

- Financial capital is money in the form of financial assets, including money in bank accounts, money loaned by investors, and obligations by others to pay money.
- Natural capital is naturally occurring in the environment and is an enriching asset for everyone. Examples are trees, water and oil.
- Human capital covers all aspects of value in human talent, knowledge and social interactions. It includes some sub-categories, such as: *social capital*, characterized by human interactions that have value, such as brand loyalty and goodwill; *instructional capital*, or *intellectual capital*, which is teaching or knowledge transfer; *individual capital*, which is made up of the valuable skills, abilities and knowledge inherent in individuals. It is closely related to labour, and some economic approaches don't distinguish between the two.

The pioneering Scottish political economist Adam Smith distinguished between fixed capital (items not used up in production, such as tools and factories) and circulating capital (items such as raw materials, which are used up in production).

The capital of a whole nation includes goods from which everyone benefits, for example, the infrastructure of roads and railways, amenities such as electricity and water supply, and publicly owned schools and hospitals.

Putting people at the centre: labour
Neoclassical economics does not make the people who provide labour a particularly important part of the equation. It puts capital at the heart of economic activity. Workers are treated, in general, as a resource which can easily be replaced or renewed, with one working unit exchangeable for another.

The German political philosopher Karl Marx (1818–83), co-author with Friedrich Engels of *The Communist Manifesto*, saw production more in terms of the use of labour than the use of capital. He defined the factors of production as labour, subjects of labour, and instruments of labour. Labour, again, is the individuals who do the work. The subjects of labour are the goods acted upon to make something (raw materials). In a coffee-processing plant, the coffee beans are the subjects of labour. The instruments of labour are the tools, buildings and machinery used to carry out the work (capital assets). In processing coffee beans, the roasters and other machines used are the instruments of labour. Marx put the value added by labour at the heart of the value of goods and services in an economy. He considered all commodities to represent 'congealed labour'.

Sticks, stones and managers

The spear-maker who makes a spear for himself uses only the freely available natural resources from the land and his own labour. If he collects a stock of suitable sticks and stones to make into spears, this collection would represent circulating capital, according to Adam Smith's definition (see page 33).

Suppose now that an individual sees the spear-maker is very good at making spears, but can only devote a short period of time to the task each day because of the need to do other things such as catch and cook food, collect water and guard children from predators. This enterprising intermediary, or 'entrepreneur', might offer to take on one of these activities (guarding the children) in exchange for a share in the extra spears the spear-maker will be able to produce. The entrepreneur then gives away one spear to a childminder to guard the children.

Now the entrepreneur has no task to perform, but has made a profit in terms of spears by acting as an intermediary between the manufacturer (spear-maker) and the service provider (childminder). This is something that modern economists call entrepreneurial capital. It is the management of an organization to make the 'best use' of its production.

Something for nothing?

Although it looks as though the entrepreneur does nothing, he/she:

> 'That part of a man's stock which he expects to afford him revenue is called his capital.'
>
> Adam Smith, *The Wealth of Nations* (1776)

- sees an opportunity
- thinks of a way of exploiting it
- sources the different parties who can work together
- vets (we hope) the childminder
- handles the payment to the childminder
- oversees to ensure that the childminder does the work competently
- supervises the quality of the spears and rate of production.

The dragon-slayers of old could go about their business with impunity thanks to the efforts of spear and lance manufacturers and, possibly, the entrepreneurs who sold the weapons on.

While the spear-maker exploits natural capital (sticks and stones), the entrepreneur exploits human capital (the spear-maker and the childminder).

The entrepreneur might act as an agent, taking a percentage of the spears produced, or as an employer, perhaps even providing the sticks and stones and allowing the spear-maker to keep a certain number of the spears as a wage. In the last scenario, the entrepreneur has become a capitalist – someone who owns the means of production and puts it to use to make a profit for themselves, paying for labour in the process.

For all we know, there might have been entrepreneurs long ago, but it is generally thought that this type of economic activity developed over time as Western societies adopted more sophisticated forms of commerce (see Chapter 6).

CHAPTER 3

How do supply and demand work?

In a free market, economics follows the law of supply and demand.

Every economy works, or fails, by a process of supplying the goods, services and resources for which there is a demand. Supply and demand are therefore the main forces acting in an economy.

The demand curve

From everyday experience we know that the demand for goods falls as price rises: we tend to buy less of something the more expensive it becomes. Economists show this relationship between the quantity people want and the price of an item by drawing a downward-sloping demand curve (although it's called a curve, it's usually a straight line).

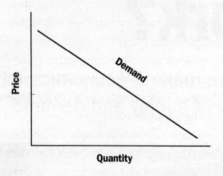

The demand curve applies to all kinds of things, not just goods for sale. It also applies to labour, for example. When the price of labour – wages – is high, the demand for workers is low. As the price falls, demand increases.

The supply curve

There is also a curve that goes in the opposite direction to show how supply varies with price. When a good can only command a low price, fewer producers will want to supply it, so the quantity supplied falls. As the price rises, more people will choose to sell it, so the supply will also rise (see facing page).

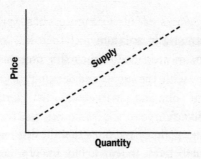

Move along

Some circumstances can cause the demand or supply curve to shift to the right or left. If people have more money (if incomes rise), the demand curve will probably shift to the right, but stay the same shape. The relationship between quantity and price is the same, but the absolute number of items sold increases at all points on the curve. Other changes can also affect the curve. A hot summer might shift the curve for beer to the right (see graph below); people will buy more beer at the same prices because they want it more. If incomes decline, the curve shifts to the left as demand falls.

The same can happen with the supply curve. If there is a bumper harvest, the supply curve for fruit will shift to the right as the price drops all along the curve. A shortage will shift the curve to the left.

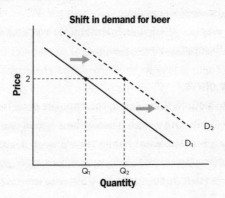

Shift in demand for beer

Supply and demand in balance

As long as goods are available at a price that some buyers and sellers are happy with, the supply and demand curves will intersect at some point and a market will exist. Plotting the supply and demand curves on the same axes (see the graph below) shows the quantity and price at which the two intersect. This will define the market for the type of goods. The same X-shaped graph can be drawn for all kinds of things that can be bought and sold.

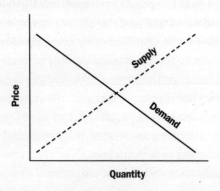

The point at which the lines intersect is called the equilibrium point and indicates how many goods are likely to be sold and the price they are likely to fetch.

Let's suppose the graph shows the supply and demand curves for pineapples. When the price of pineapples is high, demand for them is low. As the price drops, the quantity demanded increases. When the price is low, few producers want to supply them, so supply is low. Between the bottom ends of the supply and demand lines there is a big gap – this represents people who would like to buy pineapples at a low price, but will be frustrated as there aren't enough available.

As the price rises (moving up the y-axis), more producers

want to supply pineapples but fewer consumers want to buy them. At the top point on the price axis, there is another big gap. This represents the glut of pineapples that would be left unsold at this price because not enough people want to buy all the pineapples the producers would like to supply.

The sweet point

At the point of equilibrium, there are enough pineapples available to satisfy demand at a price enough people can afford to pay and at which suppliers can afford to produce them. If more pineapples were produced they would remain unsold as supply would outstrip demand at this price. The shaded area in the graph below represents the pineapples that could not be sold if the quantity produced increased to Q.

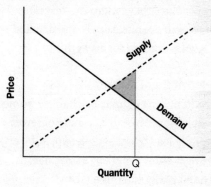

Any market will naturally gravitate towards the equilibrium point unless it is prevented from doing so or is artificially altered (by a government subsidy on production, for example).

The point of equilibrium is also called the market-clearing point, as it is the point at which the whole quantity supplied should be sold, leaving the market clear, with no disappointed buyers and no sellers encumbered with goods they can't sell. In practice, the equilibrium is not stable; frequent changes in supply, demand and price cause it to shift.

Supply, demand and competition

Competition for scarce resources affects price, and is clearly related to the supply and demand curves. If there are more workers available than jobs, the supply of workers is greater than the demand and there is competition for jobs. This (in theory) will push wages down. If there are plenty of jobs and not enough workers, the supply of labour is too low and there is competition for workers. Wages will rise as employers compete to attract workers.

If there is a scarcity of a product that people want, such as sugar or gas, its price rises; people are competing for it and willing to pay more than usual. If there is more of a product than people want to buy, its price goes down. The relationship can be used to manipulate markets. If governments want more people to borrow money, they reduce interest rates. The idea is that market forces will operate: supply and demand will adjust until the right level is reached for everything.

Entering and leaving the market

The supply of an item can't usually be changed immediately just because people would like to buy more or fewer. Changes in demand generally lead to changes in supply, by encouraging producers to leave or enter a market. Sometimes this can happen quickly and easily, but often it can't.

When there are very few pineapples available, demand outstrips supply. This creates competition and the price of pineapples rises. In terms of the supply curve on page 41, at the left-hand side, quantity is low (the x-axis) and price is high (the y-axis). This is good for suppliers of pineapples, but not for consumers. At this point other traders will enter the market as they see an opportunity to make money by supplying pineapples to satisfy demand. The supply now increases. But not enough people will be willing to pay a very high price for pineapples, so to sell the surplus now available the price has to come down.

If lots of new suppliers enter the pineapple market, there will be oversupply. This is the right-hand side of the graph. There are now more pineapples than people want so to sell them the suppliers have to drop the price considerably. If the price goes too low, some suppliers will not be able to afford to deal in pineapples and will leave the market. Supply then decreases, so the price can rise again. The market finds a new equilibrium.

Moving curves

If a market reaches an equilibrium point and the price of the item changes, the equilibrium will move along the demand curve. If the price of an item goes up, it is likely that fewer items will be sold; if the price goes down, it is likely that more will sell.

This can happen when external circumstances have an impact on a market. For example, if the market for pineapples was at equilibrium but then a hurricane destroyed much of the crop, the supply would fall, but the price would not have changed (though it might subsequently change).

There are also seasonal changes in the supply of/demand for some goods. Raspberries are more plentiful during the summer, so they tend to be cheaper during this season. In winter, raspberries have to be imported. The supply is lower, the cost higher, therefore the price is higher. Fewer people want to pay the higher price for raspberries in the winter, so a new supply/demand equilibrium is found.

Economics and people

On paper, it's clear: if too few people want to buy pineapples, supply will adjust until the right number of pineapples is produced for them all to sell at a price that makes pineapple farming profitable. What this ignores is the human cost: the 'surplus' farmers forced into poverty, possibly along a path of anxiety, depression and despair, not knowing whether to stay with pineapples or switch to growing something else on their now unprofitable land. Farmers probably have not wilfully set out to farm pineapples in a saturated market. They will have started when pineapples were in demand, or when production methods were less efficient and the market was not yet flooded, or perhaps because they were offered government incentives to farm pineapples.

And even though 'labour' is a market, labour is provided by people, and people produce all the goods and services we buy.

ADAM SMITH (1723–90)

Adam Smith was a Scots philosopher and pioneer of political economy. In 1776, he published *An Inquiry into the Nature and Causes of the Wealth of Nations* (usually called *The Wealth of Nations*), the first modern text on economics. He set out the basis of free-market economics and explained how 'rational self-interest' and competition produce wealth and prosperity in an economy. In the first account of competition in markets, he explained how it led to the most productive allocation of resources. If a set of raw materials, workers and investment could be used in several different ways, competition would ensure that the most profitable use of them predominated. Smith is famous for citing an 'invisible hand' working to promote the benefit of society from the self-interested actions of individuals:

'Every individual . . . intends only his own gain, and he is in this, as in many other cases, led by an invisible hand to promote an end which was not part of his intention.'

Ethical economics needs to take account of people as well as numbers in its application. At this point, economics becomes political. In some areas of production, initiatives such as 'fair trade' are put in place to protect producers in the developing world from the worst aspects of trading in often rapacious global markets.

Not that simple

In theory, markets will naturally gravitate towards the equilibrium price but, in practice, other factors often intervene and market forces are not strong enough to overcome them. Consequently, the optimal balance of supply and demand is not always (perhaps seldom) achieved.

Markets don't exist in isolation and people don't always act rationally. People in the developed world can easily get by without pineapples; they are a luxury, not a staple. How many people buy will be affected by the market for alternatives – other types of fruit, for example. If all other fruit rose in price, pineapples would seem comparatively cheap and more people would choose to buy them. But other factors could affect people's choice, including:

- a health scare which suggested that pineapples are contaminated with pesticides
- a popular TV chef promoting a recipe involving pineapple
- concern for the wellbeing of workers on pineapple farms
- a news story suggesting that pineapples are very good for your health
- a suggestion that eating pineapples is cool.

Ironically, even a rise in the price of pineapples could increase demand if people wanted the kudos of being seen to eat an expensive and therefore 'exclusive' item.

Time matters

If demand for a product changes, the supply is likely to change to match it. But suppliers need to know whether a change in demand is a long-term trend or a short-term fad. For example, if one winter is particularly wet, the demand for wellington boots might increase. One rainy season is not going to attract more bootmakers into the market, however; it will take longer than that to set up a new factory to make boots. It is likelier that businesses already making boots will increase production by paying overtime to existing staff and/or taking on casual workers. But if higher levels of rainfall become the norm, more bootmakers will be attracted into the market. The guaranteed long-term increase in sales of wellington boots will make it worthwhile for new firms to set up in business, and for existing producers to expand to meet the new demand.

Inferior goods

If they can afford it, people generally like to buy things of a reasonable quality. If they can't afford it, they may be forced to buy lower quality items. These are known as inferior goods. An example would be cheaply made clothes available from high street discount stores. The demand curve for inferior goods doesn't follow the usual pattern of shifting to the right as income increases. When people can afford to buy goods of better quality, they do so – the market for inferior goods decreases (the curve shifts to the left) as income increases.

Elasticity of demand

The extent to which a change in a product's price affects supply and demand is known as 'price elasticity'. If a product is highly elastic, any change in its price will lead to a big change in demand, and any change in supply will have a large impact on price.

This is most likely to be the case with goods for which substitutes are readily available. For example, if apple juice goes up in price, many people will switch to other fruit juices. A price rise of 10 per cent might lead to a drop in demand of 20 per cent or more. Demand is considered to be price elastic if a percentage change in price brings about a larger percentage change in demand; it is inelastic if it brings about a smaller percentage change in demand.

Some goods are inelastic in the short term, but elastic in the long term. This happens if making a sudden switch to another product is impractical. For example, even if oil prices were to double tomorrow, consumers would still have to fill their petrol tanks. They might cut back on non-essential journeys, but most would still use their cars for essential travel. So demand might fall, but it would not halve. If the change was clearly going to be long term, it would slowly lead to a permanent shift in demand, as people switched to more economical vehicles or public transport. Vehicle manufacturers would develop more fuel-efficient alternatives. In the long term, therefore, the price rise would have a more significant effect on demand.

Lots of markets

An economy comprises many markets for many different products. All of them follow the same laws of supply and demand and are interlinked. Sometimes the link is obvious: if the supply of steel is reduced, the supply of cars made from steel will also decrease and the price of cars will go up. Some are less obviously linked. If demand for beef increases, the price of beef will go up and supply will increase as beef producers seek to capitalize on the increased market for their product.

At the same time, more leather will be produced as a by-product of the increased beef production. The supply of leather will increase, with no corresponding increase in demand, so its price will drop.

The labour market

There is a market for labour (the work provided by employees), just as there is a market for goods and services. If there is a large number of workers available, perhaps because of a rise in unemployment or an influx of cheap labour, wages will be lower. In times of high employment, when labour is scarce, employers will have to pay higher wages to attract workers.

Again, the model of the supply and demand curves is a simplification. There might be high unemployment in general, but a scarcity of workers with a particular skill, such as trained nurses. Unemployed people can't suddenly retrain to take up the vacant posts. A situation that is familiar in many industrial countries at the moment is an oversupply of unskilled or semi-skilled workers, but a shortage of workers with the specialist skills required. So there is a shortfall in skilled people, but a surplus of workers in general.

In some industries, there are always more people seeking work than there are jobs available for them. For example, there is never a shortage of people wanting to be footballers, actors, writers, singers or artists. Many people who would like such a job also have the necessary talents, but there are not enough jobs to go round. Consequently most people working in these industries are poorly paid because the oversupply means that they are easily replaced.

CHAPTER 4

Does cost reflect value?

The price label on an item in a shop only gives an indication of the cost of production.

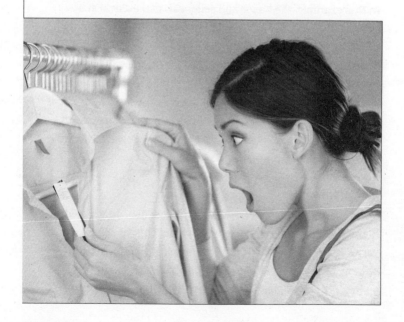

In daily life, the price of goods and services is generally set by the market. The value and cost of an item are related in complex ways, reflected in the price.

Buyers and sellers

If you go to a street market where you can haggle over prices, or buy items on online auction sites, you will already be used to the idea that the value of an item is fluid. It depends on what a buyer is willing to pay and what a seller is willing to accept for it. Generally, buyer and seller will accept a range of prices; as long as these prices coincide (or intersect) at some point, a deal can be made.

0	1	2	3	4	5	6	7
will buy							
			will sell				

In this example, the buyer and seller can make a deal at a price between $3 and $4.99. Below $3, the seller is unwilling to sell; at $5 or above, the buyer is unwilling to buy. The value of an item lies between the most and the least it can be sold for. Economists distinguish between these values. The value placed on a good or service by the buyer is the most he or she is willing to pay for it, and represents its economic value. At the other end of the scale, the market value is the lowest price at which the seller can be certain to sell.

Economic value

The measure of the benefit or utility that something provides to the buyer is known as economic value. This, of course, varies from one buyer to another and according to different circumstances, but the average tends to determine the price of an item. For example, suppose a small bottle of drinking water usually sells for $1. At a music festival on a hot day, bottled water could easily sell for $2 a bottle, as people are thirsty and have no other recourse to water. But on a cold winter's day, it may be impossible to sell bottled water at all.

Neoclassical economics considers the economic value of an item to be the price it will command in a 'perfect, competitive market' – so it is equivalent to the prevailing price.

Market value

Market value is generally lower than economic value. It is the minimum price a consumer could pay for something. For sellers, market value is the price they can expect an item to fetch. It's possible that they might sell the item for less than they would like, but it must still be economic to manufacture, market and ship the item for its market value, or they will not make any profit.

Bread with no butter

The value of items and the market for them are rarely entirely independent of other factors. For example, if there is a bread shortage, demand for butter and other spreads (and therefore their market value) is likely to fall to some extent. Consumers' ability to pay for something also depends on how much money they have. For example, rent and mortgage payments are bills which must be paid, so if these rise people will have less money to spend on non-essential things. The demand for, and market value of, non-essential items might then fall.

Substitute and complementary goods

The supply, demand and price curves of some goods are linked.

Substitute goods are those which can replace another good: if the price of pasta goes up, or the supply is restricted, sales of rice as a substitute good might increase.

THE PERFECT MARKET

Economists often use the idea of a 'perfect, competitive market', meaning a market with competition at the highest degree and no distorting factors. The perfect market is defined by the following:

- all participants have perfect knowledge of all conditions
- producers and consumers make rational decisions to maximize their self-interest (utility for consumers and profit for producers)
- producers and consumers can freely enter and leave the market at any time
- all items of output are identical and interchangeable
- all units of input, including workers, are identical and interchangeable
- there are many firms in the market
- no single firm can influence the market price, or market conditions
- there is no government regulation
- there are no external costs or benefits
- firms can only make normal profits in the long run

This situation is never possible, however, as real markets are too varied, complex and changing.

Complementary goods are those bought alongside one another, so the supply, demand and price curves of one affect the sale of the other.

If the supply of pasta drops, the sale of pasta sauces will also fall as they are usually only used with pasta. It works the other way round, too. If the price of cinema tickets drops, the sale of popcorn in cinema foyers will rise as people will be going to the cinema more.

Cost of production

For a supplier, such as a manufacturer or a farmer, the value of an item can be measured in terms of what it has cost to produce. If the supplier is going to succeed in business, they must recover the cost of production. To make a profit, the business needs to make more from the sale of the goods than they cost to produce.

> **MARGINAL UTILITY**
>
> The value of an item is not the same each time you buy it. The change in utility (satisfaction) that you get with each additional item of a certain type is called its marginal utility. If you are hungry, you'll get high marginal utility from eating a sandwich. But you'll get less marginal utility from eating a second sandwich. At this point, you probably won't want any more. If you are then forced to have a third sandwich you don't want, you'll gain negative marginal utility from the extra sandwich.

The cost of production is the total cost of raw materials, capital used in making the goods (land, equipment and so on) and the cost of the labour, including the producer's own labour, in making and marketing the goods.

Suppose someone makes bespoke rocking horses at the rate of one a week. The raw materials (wood, paint, varnish, leather, metal parts) cost $70. She pays $100 a week rent for a workshop. The cost of her equipment, averaged over its lifetime, is $20 a week (see box on page 54). Other running costs, such as electricity, advertising, and so on come to $30 a week. She doesn't employ anyone else and values her own labour at $700 a week. So she must sell each rocking horse for at least $920 (70 + 100 + 20 + 30 + 700) or she will make a loss. In fact, she sets the price of each rocking horse at $1,100, representing $920 costs plus $180 profit.

Value for consumers

For consumers, value is set by the benefit they hope to gain from an item. This takes account of opportunity cost (what they have given up in order to buy the item). In choosing a rocking horse, consumers decide whether they (or their children) will get sufficient extra pleasure from a handmade rocking horse to justify spending $1,100 rather than buying a factory-made one from a high street store for under $100. If they bought the cheap rocking horse, they would have an extra $1,000 to spend on other things.

Many consumers can't afford an expensive rocking-horse, so the question does not arise. Some feel the beauty of the handmade item is worth the extra money, or hope to pass it on to future generations, or hope it will be an investment. A few will be able to afford it without worrying about the cost. Those who buy at this price set the value of the utility they will gain from the rocking horse at $1,100.

DEPRECIATING CAPITAL

Capital goods that wear out are subject to depreciation – the amount their value decreases over time. Manufacturers have to take the depreciation of capital goods into account when they consider the cost of producing goods. Even though the goods might last a long time, the cost of buying, repairing, servicing and eventually replacing them must be included in the projection. Suppose it costs $1 million to equip a factory with the machinery to make plastic combs. The factory makes five million combs a year and the machinery lasts 20 years before it needs to be replaced. The cost of the machinery is spread over its lifetime so that $1 million, divided between 100 million combs (5 million x 20 years), is 1 cent per comb. That must be taken into account, along with all the other costs, when setting a price per comb.

Measuring utility

Some economists try to measure utility in purely financial terms. The aesthetic benefit of owning a beautiful object does not count for anything in this scheme. It gives valuations that look odd and far from market values.

Suppose a biology student spends $75 on a textbook, but decides not to continue with biology so never puts it to use. By the time he decides to dispose of it, the book has been superseded and has no resale value ($0). He gives it to a charity shop, which puts it on sale for $1. A teenager buys the book. It inspires her to change course and study biology and she earns $50,000 more over her lifetime as a consequence. To her, the book has brought $50,000 of utility, so it is very valuable. So what then is the value of the book? $0, $1, $75, or $50,000?

All that work

Another way of calculating value was first suggested by Adam Smith and adopted by Karl Marx. It calculates the value of an object in terms of the labour involved in producing it. This is called the labour theory of value (LTV). It measures the value of all the labour involved in the production of a good or service, including the labour needed to make the capital involved. In calculating the LTV of, say, hairdryers, it is necessary to include figures for a share of building the machinery and the factories involved, for designing the electronics, running the canteen in the factory, producing plastic from oil, and so on. LTV is a feature of heterodox economics.

Use value and exchange value

Marx distinguished between use value and exchange value. Use value is a measure of how useful things are to us – the amount of utility or benefit they bring. Exchange value is the value we place on one thing in comparison to others. Typically we think of exchange values in terms of money: we can exchange $10 for a book, for example, or for a meal in a café. The book and the meal have the same exchange value.

Bubbles

Like most economic theory, the balance between use value and exchange value depends on people acting rationally in ideal market conditions. But people don't always act rationally. In economic 'bubbles', people pay inflated prices for goods because they think they will increase in value. When the value falls, people are left with worthless belongings. The 'dotcom bubble' of the 1990s saw this phenomenon, with shares in internet-based companies rocketing. Investors saw others making fortunes online so bought shares indiscriminately, including in businesses without a sound business plan and with no prospect of success. As a result, these businesses were massively over-valued and quickly went bust.

One of the most bizarre and catastrophic examples of people acting irrationally in relation to value occurred in the 17th century. Tulips were introduced to the Netherlands from Turkey in 1593 and soon became popular. Then, in the early 1600s, a virus affected the tulips, causing coloured flares to appear on the petals. The infected tulips were regarded as more attractive, so commanded a higher price. As the fad for tulips flourished, so did prices. In one month, the price of tulips rose twentyfold. Convinced that the value would continue to increase, people who were not tulip-traders began to invest in tulip bulbs.

At the height of the craze, speculators spent their entire life savings on tulips, or sold a house to buy a single bulb. One bulb changed hands for 5,200 florins. When the bottom fell out of the market, the principal investors were hit very hard and some were ruined. It was the first commodity boom and crash, but certainly not the last. During the period of so-called 'tulip mania' the use value of tulips was disregarded and the

exchange value became monstrously inflated. A combination of greed and panic fuelled a boom in trade that could not last, simply because the difference between use and exchange values had grown so large so quickly.

How much for those beanies?

The bubble phenomenon can be deliberately exploited. In the 1990s, many people bought 'beanie babies' – small plush toys made by a company called Ty. A clever marketing strategy persuaded people that beanie babies would become valuable, so were an investment. Ty made many different designs, but kept each one available for only a limited time, then 'retired' it and released a new design. In this way they engineered scarcity so that the exchange value of the toys would increase – which it did. 'Retired' beanie babies changed hands for hundreds of dollars. The exchange value of beanie babies was artificially and ridiculously high, while the use value was very low. There are many people today with boxes of these toys. The 'value' of beanie babies existed only in the bubble of the market.

Other measures of value

We have focused on measuring value in terms of money or exchange value, partly because there is no other universally accepted measure. Some economists have tried to measure utility value in nominal, artificial units called 'utils', but it doesn't work very well. We could say that a chair is worth 40 utils and a car is worth 5,000 utils, but the comparison is rather arbitrary. If you only need a car, a chair has no use value to you at all, and vice versa.

Another way of measuring value, applicable in some circumstances, is time. We all have a finite amount of time, both in a day and in our lives. Whether we are expending it on an activity, or simply waiting, it will have a cost in time. For example, would you prefer to pay more to have something delivered to your home rather than go to a shop to buy it? Would you be prepared to wait in a long queue simply to buy something more cheaply? Alternatively, would you be happy to spend more on an item you could buy locally because you value your time more than the amount it would cost to travel further to get it?

'The real price of everything, what everything really costs to the man who wants to acquire it, is the toil and trouble of acquiring it. What everything is really worth to the man who has acquired it, and who wants to dispose of it, or exchange it for something else, is the toil and trouble which it can save to himself, and which it can impose upon other people. That this is really the foundation of the exchangeable value of all things, excepting those which cannot be increased by human industry, is a doctrine of the utmost importance in political economy.'

Adam Smith, *The Wealth of Nations* (1776)

As we have seen, scarcity can bestow value and can even be manipulated to make things with low intrinsic or utility value and little lasting exchange value seem valuable. A piece of art appears to be a safe investment. Surely works by a great – but deceased – artist will always keep their value, as these are in short supply and each one is unique? But fashions and tastes in art change, and the work of an artist who has fallen out of favour may fall in value, even though the paintings themselves remain unchanged.

CHAPTER 5

How do we know if a country is rich or poor?

Do you live in a rich country?
Measuring the comparative wealth
of countries is a tricky process.

If someone asked you how much money you have, you might think of the cash in your pocket or the total money deposited in your bank account. You might also include the value of your possessions, at least the big ones, such as your house and car. If you own stocks and shares, those are also part of your wealth. Another way of thinking of your wealth is in terms of income. Similarly, when referring to wealthy nations, we can take account of the country's reserves (its stock of money, gold and other assets) and its income. Generally, income is more important.

Wealth of nations

In the case of nations, there is a strong correlation between wealth and income. Economists consider wealth to be a stock of assets that produces income. On the whole, nations are less likely than individuals to leave valuable assets languishing; they are likely to put them to work to generate income. It is reasonable, then, that the wealth of nations is usually compared by estimating their levels of income.

TANGIBLE AND INTANGIBLE ASSETS

An asset is anything that has value. Assets can be tangible, such as buildings and money, or intangible, such as copyright in a piece of music or the right to extract oil from a piece of ground. Tangible assets are physical objects, whereas intangible assets have no physical existence.

A country's income is often reported in terms of Gross Domestic Product (GDP). This is a measure of the value of everything a nation produces. It works from the final value of goods and services, so it includes taxes on spending, such as value added tax (VAT).

Calculating GDP

The figures for GDP are calculated from millions of tax returns and other documents collected by governments. They are never fully accurate; some people make mistakes in returns, and some don't complete them honestly (or at all).

There are also types of 'product' that are not bought and sold. In the UK, for instance, healthcare is funded by the government – the patient pays nothing other than a charge for prescribed medicines from a pharmacy. Only 10 per cent of prescriptions attract even that charge. Medicines, surgical procedures and care in hospital are 'free at the point of use' for UK nationals. This means that most of the output of the National Health Service (NHS) would not show up in GDP unless there was another way of accounting for it. The solution is to include the cost to the government of providing healthcare in GDP as income (the value of services produced) from the NHS.

How better can be worse

One oddity resulting from accounting for productivity by looking at cost is that if a service becomes more efficient and costs less to deliver, it looks as though less has been produced. Suppose nurses take on some tasks previously carried out by doctors. Nurses are paid less than doctors, so the cost of providing the treatment falls even though the same number of patients are being treated. An improvement in efficiency (a good thing) looks like a fall in productivity (a bad thing) with this form of accounting.

What's missing?

GDP only includes goods and services that are declared. This means the hidden (or 'black') economy doesn't feature in GDP, nor do goods and services for which no money changes hands.

The hidden economy describes informal exchanges that seek to avoid taxation through undeclared cash transactions. If a householder pays cash to a gardener to mow the lawn, or to a bricklayer to construct a wall, there may be no official paper trail of the work or the payment. Self-employed workers who are paid in cash might choose to declare only part (or even none) of their income to the tax authorities. In this way, they avoid paying taxes. This is, of course, illegal, and difficult to monitor. Electronic bank transfers and cheque payments leave a trace that the tax authorities can find, but cash does not. There are other reasons for not declaring income. Someone may wish to continue claiming welfare benefits which would be removed if the claimant's true income was known (also illegal). Or the income may be from an illegal activity, such as drug dealing, which can't be declared for fear of prosecution.

Doing it for yourself

Not everything missing from GDP is illegal or fraudulent. Much work produces no accountable income, but does generate value. Anyone who undertakes a do-it-yourself (DIY) home refurbishment project or grows their own fruit and vegetables has generated a valuable product they might otherwise have paid for. Childcare, looking after older relatives and household chores are services often provided for free within families. In some parts of the world, people engage in subsistence farming, so they grow food solely for their own families to eat rather than for selling to the public. This does not appear in the GDP of the country, but is an important source of value for the population.

Uses of GDP

Economists use GDP as a measure of the standard of living in a country. By comparing current GDP with previous years, they gain an idea of how the standard of living has improved or deteriorated. By comparing the GDP of different countries, economists can rank them in order of prosperity and living standards.

Comparing GDP over time

If the GDP of a nation increases over time, it suggests living standards are improving. However, inflation has to be taken into account (see Chapter 14). Inflation is a sustained rise in general prices over time. This means that during a period of inflation the same sum of money is exchanged for less in terms of goods and services. If the GDP of a nation rises from $200 billion to $210 billion over a period of five years (a rise of 5 per cent) but prices rise 10 per cent over that period, the standard of living will fall – the $210 billion represents less in terms of goods and services than the original $200 billion. To avoid inflation skewing the results, economists distinguish between nominal GDP and real GDP. Nominal GDP is the calculated figure, not taking prices into account. Real GDP is corrected to take account of the retail price index, so is more useful for comparative purposes.

Another factor not shown by GDP is population size. If the GDP of a nation increases by 5 per cent over a period, but the population increases by 10 per cent, there will be a fall in average living standards because each person will have a smaller share of GDP. We can take account of this by calculating and comparing per capita GDP – that is, GDP divided by the population.

Still not right

There are some problems that calculating per capita GDP does not address. Just as increased efficiency can look like a drop in productivity, so can an increase in quality if it comes at no extra cost. The true cost of electronic goods has fallen over the last few decades while their speed, quality and storage capabilities have increased many times. In 2015, the sale of a computer for $500 shows up in GDP as less valuable than a computer sold for $1,000 in 1990. But the 2015 computer will be much more powerful than the earlier model. Also, scarcity can raise prices. If the price of oil doubles and consumption falls by a quarter, spending on oil has increased; this means GDP increases, but productivity and standards of living fall.

Rising GDP apparently suggests a rising standard of living, but this is not always the case. Increases in public spending add to GDP, but, in reality, some might mean a fall in the standard of living. During wartime, spending on defence is very high. This shows up in the country's accounts as a rise in GDP, but people might be enduring a much lower standard of living than they were in peacetime. Similarly, civil unrest or high crime rates might lead to increased spending on policing, again raising GDP – yet people have a lower standard of living when plagued by riots, crime and falling bombs.

Even very high GDP might not reflect a good standard of living for most people if there is great inequality in a country. Rising GDP can be accounted for by a small wealthy class spending extravagantly, while the majority of people have a falling standard of living (see Chapter 15).

Splurging

If you took out all your savings and bought new furniture and clothes, ate in expensive restaurants and took foreign holidays, you would enjoy a high standard of living now, but the future would be bleak unless you could replace the money. It's the same for nations, which need to balance investment and consumption. If a nation spends all its money in the short term and doesn't invest, GDP will rise immediately, but will almost certainly be lower later on. In democratic countries, governments are elected to serve for a limited term, so need to attract voters. The temptation to 'spend now and pay later' can be considerable and means that the financial consequences of a spending programme might not be felt until the next government is in power.

Mine is bigger than yours

GDP is often used to compare the standard of living or wealth between two or more nations. Again, it's important to take account of the population to calculate per capita GDP. Otherwise, if we work just with total GDP, a country with a small, wealthy population may look worse off than a country with a very large, poor population.

Whose currency?

One difficulty with comparing national economies is deciding which currency to use. If the GDP of the UK is reported in pounds sterling (£), that of Eurozone countries in euros (€) and that of the USA in dollars ($), how can they be compared? The exchange rate fluctuates and, if one currency is particularly strong (or weak) on the day the comparison is made, it may give a distorted picture of the relative wealth of the countries.

CHANGING GDP

A simple equation allows economists to work out how long it will take to double or halve GDP, given a rate of change.

If the rate of increase is g per cent, it will take 70/g years for GDP to double.

If the rate of increase is 3.5 per cent, it will take 70 ÷ 3.5 = 20 years for GDP to double.

If the rate of change is 2 per cent, it will take 70 ÷ 2 = 35 years for GDP to double.

Instead, international dollars, (Int$), are often used. These are also called the Geary–Khamis dollar, named after Roy Geary and Salem Hanna Khamis, the economists who proposed and developed the idea. The international dollar is equivalent in terms of purchasing power to the US$ at a specified moment in time, often 1999 or 2000.

Here are some figures for national GDP for the year 2014, taken from the International Monetary Fund's data:

Country	Per capita GDP, Int $	Ranking
Qatar	143,427	1
Luxembourg	92,049	2
Norway	66,937	6
USA	54,597	10
Australia	46,433	15
Germany	45,888	18
Canada	44,843	20
France	40,375	24
UK	39,511	27
Japan	37,390	28
New Zealand	35,152	31
Russia	24,805	49
Mexico	17,881	66
South Africa	13,046	87
India	5,855	125
Bangladesh	3,373	142
Niger	1,048	182
Central African Republic	607	187

In April 2015, the per capita GDP of the whole world was Int$15,147.

DIY disruption

Cultural patterns affect GDP in a way that makes meaningful comparison difficult. Domestically produced goods (DIY, growing vegetables, childcare, for example) can be particularly disruptive in comparing the GDP of different nations.

If we examine the per capita GDP of some economies, it looks as though they should not be sustainable. How can the Central African Republic survive, if production is Int$607 per year (less than Int$2 a day) per person? But in the Central African Republic many people produce food and other goods for themselves. These figures don't show up in the formal economy and therefore do not appear in GDP.

If a farmer hatches chicks from her hens and raises more chickens for meat and eggs, which she either eats or barters with neighbours for other goods, this productivity is not recognized in the international financial markets. Yet the amount a person in the USA spends on eggs and chicken – and other items the African farmer has bartered for – might represent several hundred dollars of GDP. It could be more than the entire per capita GDP of the Central African Republic.

Even if you grew lots of vegetables, built your own house and kept chickens, it would be pretty hard to survive in the USA on the average income of a resident of the Central African Republic. This is because things cost a lot more in the USA, and there are more necessary expenses such as heating, lighting and transport. The relative costs of items in different countries are compared using purchasing power parity (see box on page 68).

Buying what's needed

The items individuals need to pay for vary with circumstances, too. Scandinavians pay a lot for heating fuel, but in Niger this level of expenditure is not necessary because the climate is much warmer. In the USA, most people have to pay for transport to get to work, but in some poorer economies most people simply walk to work. In the USA, most people pay for healthcare through health insurance, but in the UK healthcare is provided by central government and paid for through taxation. All these differences affect standards of living and comparisons between countries. If you don't need to buy as much, you don't need to earn as much.

PURCHASING POWER PARITY

Purchasing power parity is a way of comparing the purchasing power (what can be bought for each unit of currency) of two different national currencies. It is calculated by comparing the prices of two identical items with the official exchange rate of the currencies. For example, if the exchange rate of Chinese yuan to euros is 7:1, for the two currencies to have equal purchasing power an item that costs 1 euro in Spain should cost 7 yuan in China. If the item costs 4 yuan, someone in China could buy more with the same amount of money, so the purchasing power of the yuan would be higher than that of the euro.

CHAPTER 6

How did we get here?

Modern economics systems have developed over a long period of time, during which they have adapted as societies have changed.

You are almost certainly reading this book in a country with a well-established economy and at least some elements of capitalism. Capitalism is an economic system based on the principle that business is run to make a profit. It's the dominant economic system in the world today. (There is more about the nature, advantages and disadvantages of capitalism in Chapter 7).

The capitalist marketplace

Capitalism posits three markets: the market for labour (people working for money); the market for goods and services (things you can buy); and the financial market (buying and selling intangible products related to money). It might seem we could get along quite well with just the first two. No one *needs* to make a profit – they just need to earn enough to buy the things they require to survive in relative comfort.

This type of system has existed in the past and still exists in some parts of the world. Each person produces things that he or she sells or trades for other things they need. Before that, each person grew or made all the things they needed. It's called subsistence living and generally takes the form of subsistence farming, when each family produces what they consume in terms of food and materials. (This type of economy is called an autarky.) For an autarky to work, we each need, say, a few chickens, part ownership of a cow, some land for growing wheat and vegetables, and timber and basic tools to make furniture.

Economy starter-kit

If you want to build an economy, you need to give people distinct tasks. This provides potential for growth. And growth means, or should mean, that everyone should have a better lifestyle.

Long ago, the specialization of labour made perfect sense. One person became really good at making woollen capes from the wool produced by another person's sheep. Someone else grew lots of vegetables. Working together, the society produced more than if everyone struggled to supply all their own needs, doing tasks they were not very good at as well as tasks at which they excelled. Money became useful at this point – an economy based on tokens is easier to manage than one based on barter (see Chapter 1).

If all went well, the society had a surplus of goods and could trade with other societies. As people travelled further afield, they found new markets and new products. When Europeans discovered South America, they found tobacco, chocolate, potatoes and tomatoes which they introduced to Europe and which became items of international trade. North American Indians found they could trade a useless tract of land such as Manhattan Island for a handful of beautiful shiny beads (the beads were not valued very highly in Europe).

Growing the economy

But a simple mercantile exchange economy like this couldn't progress very far, which meant the society itself couldn't make much progress. While everyone was making or growing things for immediate sale or consumption, there was no capacity for research and development. Who would have the time to design a steam engine? Who would have the money to build a rail network? In developing economies today, there are many small-scale entrepreneurs and self-employed people, but they can't develop their businesses without capital.

Capitalism facilitates larger-scale, longer-term projects. Research and development, and expansion in manufacturing or service enterprises, all need investment. This involves being less economically productive in the short term, while developing products or doing research in order to be more economically productive in the long run. Unless someone can save the money an enterprise needs for such a venture, they must borrow it. And why would anyone lend money (which they could lose if it all went wrong) unless they stand to gain something? So a system developed in which investors lent money to businesses in the hope of getting more back in return. To reimburse them, the businesses had to make a profit.

Again and again: division of labour

So we have the three markets: labour, goods and services, and finance. One of the ways in which production can be made more efficient is by the division of labour. A single individual carrying out a complex, multi-stage task is not as productive as a group of people each undertaking part of the task and doing that same part repeatedly. This can only happen when someone takes an overview of a process and decides to increase productivity by splitting the task into more efficient

PIN MONEY

Economist Adam Smith used the example of manufacturing pins to show how the division of labour can make a business profitable. Far beyond the separation of growing, processing and weaving wool between different tradespeople, Smith suggested that a simple procedure such as making pins from wire could be broken into stages, and each stage carried out by a different worker. He claimed that whereas a worker making pins from start to finish could complete 20 pins a day, ten workers each specializing in one or two stages could, between them, make 48,000 pins a day. In 1832, pin factories were producing 8,000 pins a day per worker (nearly double the 1776 rate), and in 1980, with considerable mechanization, they made 800,000 pins a day per worker.

units. The process then needs organizing so that part-made products can be passed on at an efficient rate: it would be inefficient if one person took just a minute to complete a task, but was held up waiting for someone else whose task took five minutes. If the division has to be unequal, more people need to be employed on the slow tasks than on the quick tasks to improve production flow.

Once tasks have been broken down into discrete units, they often become easier to mechanize. Many factory jobs that involve simple tasks such as assembling or welding components have been taken over by machinery.

From feudalism to merchants

The economic system in medieval Europe was known as feudalism. Serfs or peasants – the poorest people in society – worked land owned by their local lord (hence the term 'landlord'). In exchange for their labour, serfs were given certain meagre benefits, such as food, shelter and protection from other lords. There was no competition, no free market

and serfs had little or no choice in who they worked for. Wealth was retained by the lords and was largely inherited (or seized in battle). It did not transfer to the serfs, no matter how hard they worked. It was hardly an equitable state of affairs.

By the Renaissance era, feudalism had given way to a mercantile style of economy, with the emergence of banks (first in Italy) and the growth of international trade. Individuals had more freedom; they were no longer serfs and (at least, in theory) had more choice over where they worked, for how much pay and at what type of job. Merchants ruled the system and made most of their money by trading goods – buying them cheaply in one market and selling them at a profit in another. Mercantilism encouraged minimal imports and maximum exports with the aim of acquiring bullion (gold and silver) from other nations. The idea rested on the principle of a fixed sum in the world economy, and one country could only gain money at the expense of another country. To protect home markets, governments introduced import controls, subsidies for home-produced goods and protectionist tariffs

THE BLACK DEATH: DEATH TO FEUDALISM?

Some economic historians claim that feudalism was ended by the Black Death, a pandemic that killed up to a third of the population of Europe and Asia in the 1340s. It killed so many labourers that huge tracts of land lay deserted, the crops rotting in the fields. Once the Black Death had passed, the surviving labourers were able to demand much better conditions in exchange for their work. Following the laws of supply and demand, the supply of labourers had fallen and demand was high, so those still in the market could secure better terms. These terms included freedom of movement, the freedom to work for a master of their choice, and better remuneration.

(charges imposed on imports to protect the home market). Modern economies adopt this strategy sometimes; both the USA and Japan limit imports in this way.

We can all get richer

From the 18th century, economic theorists such as David Hume and Adam Smith challenged the idea that the total wealth of the world was fixed and in the 19th century Britain abandoned its protectionist system of tariffs. The Industrial

> '[The prevention of poverty requires the] opening and well-balancing of trade; the cherishing of manufacturers; the banishing of idleness; the repressing of waste and excess by sumptuary laws; the improvement and husbanding of the soil; [and] the regulation of prices.'
>
> Francis Bacon, *Of Seditions and Troubles* (1625)

Industrialization led to an increase in child labour in the early 19th century. Starting from age ten, many children were employed in factories and coalmines, doing work that was both dirty and dangerous.

Revolution brought proper capitalism with it – archetypal capitalist factory owners who 'ground the faces of the workers into the dirt' (pretty much literally). In the early years, with no legislation to protect workers, abuses were rampant. Some of the Western nations still had child labour; it was definitely not a good time and place to be at the bottom of the hierarchy. The 'dark Satanic mills' of England mentioned by William Blake in his poem 'And did those feet in ancient time' (1808) belong to this period. From the late 19th century, legislation was introduced to give more protection to the vulnerable.

HOW TO GET RICHER

It seems inconceivable that we could all get richer without someone else getting poorer, but it's possible if productivity increases. By adopting more efficient systems of production, we can produce more from the same inputs, and this generates prosperity. It works even at a personal level. If you have $5 and buy a fish to cook, you have one meal. If you spend $5 on a fishing rod, you might catch lots of fish dinners. Similarly, you could spend $5 on one bag of apples or $5 on an apple tree sapling, which would give you years of apple crops.

CHAPTER 7

Is the whole world capitalist now?

A nation seldom has the opportunity to design its economy from the ground up.

When America formed its constitution, it brought from Europe many ideas about statecraft and economics that became enshrined in the new nation state, and a free market economy was one of them.

Free-market and command economies

A free-market economy operates in the ways we have seen so far: individuals and firms own capital and use it in combination with labour, land and resources to produce goods and services. These are sold on the open market for whatever price they can command, following the rules of supply and demand. The market – the willingness of people to buy and sell – determines what will be produced, for whom, and how.

The opposite of a free-market economy is a command economy. In this, the government or state owns the capital and decides what will be produced, how it will be produced, the price at which it will be sold, and to whom it will be sold. Command economies are associated with communist countries such as the former USSR, Cuba, China and North Korea.

The principal distinction between free and command economies is ownership of the means of production. In a free-market economy, the means of production are held by individuals and firms (which are themselves owned by individuals, either in their entirety or through shareholdings). In a command economy,

the government owns the means of production on behalf of
the people.

All's fair – or not

In an ideal world, a command economy that is run benignly
should produce a fair and equitable state. In the real world,
this has not been found to happen. A concentration of wealth,
through corruption and self-interest, appears with the
emerging ruling class. At the bottom end of the scale, workers
suffer shortages and have little choice over what they can buy,
what to do with their time, and how they live.

When the government controls production and there is
no competition between producers, there is no incentive to
provide a wide choice of goods. Indeed, producing a wide
choice of goods is economically foolhardy because effort is
duplicated and production becomes less efficient. Why run
two factories producing different styles of car when you could
run one slightly larger factory producing only one style of car?
Without private owners who are keen to make a profit from
selling their model, there is no incentive to improve the single
model of car to attract more customers.

Lack of competition leads to poor standards and uniformity.
This is what happened in the communist command economies
of Eastern Europe in the years after World War II. As the
people saw the variety and quality of goods in Western
markets, they became increasingly dissatisfied with what
their own command economy could provide. Many people
wanted to leave to seek a better standard of living, and the
communist regimes had to police their borders to prevent
mass defection to the West.

On the positive side, a command economy can (if properly
run) make high-quality healthcare and education available to
all. The processes in the USSR for identifying children with

talent in sport and music, for instance, and tutoring them intensively at no cost to their parents, led to some triumphs of achievement. (Again, lack of choice has its downside – we don't know how many chosen children were coached and then rejected, or coached when they would rather not have been.)

One and all

A command economy has little space for individuality. A person with a bright idea, talent or entrepreneurial spirit can't put it to use to increase their personal wealth – it can only be used for the benefit of society as a whole. That is not necessarily a bad thing, and different societies have different ways of evaluating and appreciating the link between the individual and society. Scientists and artists in the USSR achieved feats every bit as great as their counterparts in free-market economies, but even in this case competition (this time with the West) spurred them on. Overall, however, the evidence of the command economies of the 20th century suggests that without the enticement of personal gain or recognition, some aspects of economic activity fall behind because people lack the motivation to improve.

The focus on equality in the communist states of the 20th century was not a direct result of the economic system, but had a detrimental impact on it. Instead of putting labour to its best use, some regimes launched an assault on intellectuals by, for example, forcing them to work on collective farms or in factories. In China and Cambodia, in particular, the war against the elite led to considerable human capital being wasted, not to mention extreme personal suffering. The result was that countries with immense natural resources and populations ended up with much lower productivity, and a much lower standard of living for most people, than could have been achieved in a free-market economy.

The other side of the fence

On the other hand, a free-market economy has its own problems. The means of production can easily become concentrated in the hands of a few, who become an elite and protect their positions and possessions aggressively. The market decides what is made and sold, for what price, and to whom. The market also decides who benefits from production. As consumers have free choice between goods of many types, they dictate what is sold: they won't buy things they don't want and they won't buy at prices they can't afford. In theory, competition between suppliers will drive prices down to an equilibrium point, while ensuring plenty of choice. In practice, it falls short of this ideal.

In the case of essential goods – housing, food, heating and water, for instance – people are forced to pay the price set by the market whether they like it or not. There is little or no competition in some energy markets, for example. A market with only one supplier is called a monopoly. It's impossible for a new water company, for instance, to enter the market in a country where mains water and sewerage are already established and privately owned. The new company would need to reach an agreement with the company supplying the infrastructure.

Mixed economies

Most economies today are mixed economies. They have a free market for luxury goods; meanwhile, public money is used to pay for some essential goods and services produced for the benefit of everyone. The services might include any or all of the following: the supply of amenities, such as water, electricity and gas; healthcare services including hospitals, family doctors and dentists; and transport, such as railways, bus networks and a national airline.

Some goods and services have to be provided by the state, even in a free-market economy. Examples are roads, the police force and the army. It is not possible to exclude some people from the benefits of protection by the police or the army, so this is available to everyone, whether or not they pay anything towards them (see Chapter 13).

MONOPOLIES AND OLIGOPOLIES

A monopoly is the market condition which is opposite to competition. In a monopoly, there is only one supplier or producer in the market and there are barriers to entry that prevent others starting up. These barriers might be financial, legal or physical. For example, the Saudi government controls the rights to extracting and selling oil in Saudi Arabia, so no other company can start up. An oligopoly exists when a few suppliers or producers control a market. It effectively controls prices; if one supplier drops their prices the others will follow to avoid losing their portion of the customers (market share).

The extent of the free market in a mixed economy varies. Healthcare and education are examples of services that can be supplied freely to all citizens, or they can be charged for. In some countries, there are both public and private versions available and people choose whether to use the free public service or pay for a private service that might (or might not) be better. The USA has more of a free-market approach to healthcare than the UK, with those who can afford it paying for private healthcare insurance and those who can't falling back on state provision. In the UK, the National Health Service promises good quality healthcare to all citizens, paid for entirely through taxation and 'free at the point of delivery'. The UK also has private healthcare provision, sometimes chosen by people who want and can afford an alternative to the state system.

We can measure how mixed or free a market is by looking at the proportion of GDP that goes on government spending. Overall, the UK has a more free-market approach than some other EU countries. The graph below shows that Germany and the UK, up to 2012, had more mixed economies than the USA. The USA is the largest free-market economy in the world. It has a low level of welfare support and public provision and high levels of social inequality (see Chapter 15). The Scandinavian countries spend a higher proportion of their national income on public goods and provide such benefits as free childcare and a higher level of environmental protection. People in Scandinavia have, on average, a higher standard of living than people elsewhere and a lower level of social inequality. All this provision is paid for by far higher taxes (see Chapter 8), leaving consumers with less choice of how to spend their money because they have less left over to spend.

Public spending as a share of GDP in selected countries Between 1980 and 2018 (%)

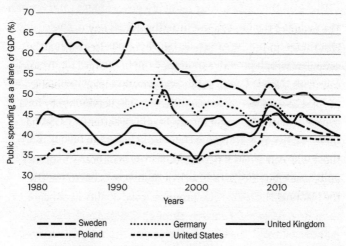

The earliest data for Poland comes from 1995; data since 2012 based on IMF projections. Source: own study on basis of IMF data.

Flavours of capitalism

Capitalism is not all one flavour, as we have seen. Laissez-faire or liberal capitalism believes in leaving as much as possible to market forces, with minimal legislation or government intervention. In the UK, this approach was favoured by the Victorian industrialists and led to extreme poverty and social inequality. Today, it is seen in many developing countries where it leads to sweatshops, child and slave labour, and terrible working conditions.

The British economist John Maynard Keynes (1883–1946) advocated a degree of government intervention in the market – even in a free-market society – to ensure that the market operates at an optimum level. This has become known as Keynesian capitalism. Western industrialized nations with mixed economies try to achieve a balance between intervention and market forces. Where exactly the right balance lies is debated by economists and is a main bone of contention between politicians on the right and left.

Those on the right favour reducing government intervention as much as possible and maximizing competition, choice and market forces on the grounds that this leads to a stronger economy which provides increased opportunities for everyone. Those on the left favour public ownership of key industries, an enlarged welfare state and increased legislation to protect consumers, workers and the disadvantaged on the grounds that a totally free market is inherently biased in favour of the employers at the expense of the workers. Most Western politicians generally try to find a middle way between these two extremes.

CHAPTER 8

Why do we pay taxes?

'Tis impossible to be sure of anything but Death and Taxes.

Christopher Bullock (1716)

Most of us grumble about taxes, and some of us expend considerable effort to avoid paying them. Yet taxes are essential if we want government to provide public goods and services – from a police force to roads and schools – the things everyone needs.

DIRECT AND INDIRECT TAXATION

Economists divide taxes into direct and indirect.

A direct tax is taken from the tax-payer when money is earned and paid straight to the government's collecting agency. Examples include income tax, collected from individuals, and corporation tax, based on the profits of businesses.

An indirect tax is collected by an intermediary, such as a retailer, at the point of sale, and passed on to the government's collecting agency later. Examples are sales tax or value added tax (VAT), usually applied as a flat percentage rate to all products, and specific excise taxes on alcohol and petrol, which vary between products.

Most economies have a mix of direct and indirect taxes. There is generally some level of taxation on income: on wages (for individuals) and profits (for businesses). This can be a flat rate tax, fixed at one level, or a progressive tax, with the level of taxation rising as income increases. There may be national and local taxes on goods and services, as in the USA. Essential items might be exempt or taxed at a lower rate. In the UK, for example, VAT is not charged on most foods, children's clothes and books.

Types of tax

Some transfers of goods or money attract additional taxes. Buying or selling land or real estate, for example, might attract stamp duty. Originally this was a charge for having the documentation of the transfer authorized – or 'stamped'. The stamp itself has gone, but the duty remains. Taxes involving the transfer of wealth are often set at a much higher rate. These include inheritance tax, on money, goods and property passed on following death, and capital gains tax, levied on the sale of high-value items, including land and real estate.

In some countries, there is a tax on valuable goods owned by individuals, such as large houses or works of art.

Tourist taxes are a way of charging for the strain put on infrastructure by a large number of visitors. Venice is an example of a city that imposes an overnight tax on visitors.

Controlling behaviour with taxes

Excise duties are taxes on the manufacture or distribution of certain types of goods. They can include import duties on goods brought in from abroad. Excise duties on luxury goods that are regarded as unhealthy are informally known as 'sin taxes'. They can be used by governments as a form of social engineering; by making the consumption of goods such as tobacco, alcohol and sugary drinks expensive, a government can discourage it.

Taxes can also be used to encourage (or 'incentivize') a particular form of behaviour. For example, a government might make sports equipment or nutritious foods exempt from sales tax to encourage a healthier lifestyle.

These taxes and exemptions to influence people's behaviour are not entirely altruistic – a healthy population is more economically productive than an unhealthy population, and requires less spending on healthcare and welfare.

Not a tax but a charge

Some levies that look like taxes are not, in economists' terms, taxes at all. In the UK, people in work pay tax on their income and they also pay National Insurance (NI) contributions.

Although NI looks like a tax (it is a percentage of income above a certain level of earnings, taken by the government) it is technically regarded as a charge for the services provided by the welfare state. These include free healthcare, welfare benefits for people who are unemployed or on low incomes, and pensions for the elderly. Compulsory payments to a local authority or utility (such as council tax in the UK) are used to fund local services such as education, refuse collection, police, and road maintenance.

WHAT CAN YOU TAX?

Some strange things have been taxed in the past.

In Ancient Rome, freedom was taxed for slaves who had earned enough to buy themselves out of slavery; so was urine (when sold for use in tanneries and other industries). In medieval Europe, there was a tax on soap.

Britain, in particular, has produced some pretty unusual taxes. During the 18th century, there was taxation on windows (if a house had more than ten), fireplaces, bricks, wig powder, candles and printed wallpaper. All these taxes were specifically targeted at the rich.

You can still see bricked up windows in some English country houses of the period, a result of trying to reduce the tax burden on the house. People tried to avoid brick taxes by using fewer and larger bricks (though these too were soon taxed at a higher rate). To avoid tax on printed wallpaper, home owners hung plain wallpaper and then painted designs onto it.

Shifting the tax burden

The amount that individuals and businesses are taxed is decided by a state's government. It often changes with a change of government and can alter during times of crisis, such as war – an expensive undertaking that needs considerable funds. The way the tax burden is allocated reflects the values of a government, and the type of economic model it favours.

A left-leaning government in a mixed economy will generally impose higher taxes (especially on the rich) so that more can be allocated to state provision (such as infrastructure and welfare). The left-wing approach favours supporting the less fortunate so that they have an acceptable standard of living, and reducing inequality. This is funded by a high level of direct taxation and sometimes higher indirect taxes on non-essential or luxury items.

A right-leaning government will tend to reduce taxes and, correspondingly, public spending. The right-wing approach favours encouraging businesses and individuals to strive by rewarding effort and profitability with high, minimally taxed income, with the aim of improving prosperity overall. Right-wing governments often charge a low level of direct taxation and a high level of indirect taxation. Indirect taxes (typically on spending) are within people's control as they can choose whether or not to spend money on items that attract taxation.

A government or local authority benefits from indirect taxation on purchases because it is not limited to residents, but must also be paid by visitors and tourists who wouldn't otherwise contribute to a country's taxation.

What's it for?
The income from taxes is spent on many essential things:

- running the process of government and the state
- enforcing law and order (policing) and national security (military)
- maintaining infrastructure (roads, canals, data cabling, public transport, and so on)

And, to varying degrees:

- funding healthcare, education and a welfare state
- running state-owned services that provide utilities such as gas, electricity and water
- funding sports facilities, museums and libraries, and the arts

WHAT'S ESSENTIAL?

In setting indirect taxation on non-essential goods, economists and politicians have to decide which goods are essential. This leads to some odd distinctions within categories.

In the UK, most food items are regarded as essential and attract no VAT. However, there is VAT on hot food, crisps, roasted, salted nuts (but not unsalted, raw nuts), biscuits (but not cakes), fruit juice (but not fruit). There is no VAT on meat, as long as it is a species usually considered to be food – therefore VAT is charged on crocodile, ostrich and horse meat. There is no VAT on 'normal' vegetables but there is on, for example, ornamental cabbages. There is no VAT on live fish of species usually eaten, but there is VAT on ornamental fish, unless they are prepared for consumption. There is VAT on animal food if the animal is not a species usually eaten by people in Britain – so there is VAT on dog food, but not on chicken feed.

Children's clothes and shoes attract no VAT. There is no VAT on a towel with a hood that can be wrapped round a baby, but there is VAT on a towel without a hood. A hat made with real fur on the outside attracts VAT, unless it is sheepskin or rabbit fur, but a hat made with artificial fur or with fur only on the inside attracts no VAT. There is no VAT on a child's scarf, but there is on scrunchies and earmuffs. There is no VAT on dressing-up outfits, including accessories such as toy guns and handcuffs, provided that they are sold as part of an entire outfit.

The income from some types of tax can be earmarked for specific services. For instance, a tax on road use could be set aside to fund road-building or public transport. This is known as ring-fencing or hypothecation.

Against taxes

Those who favour a free-market economy are often opposed to taxation because it reduces people's choice of how to spend their money. They believe that taxation distorts the market. This is because the way in which taxes are spent is decided by the government and might not reflect an individual's preferences. For example, childless citizens would probably not choose to spend money on children's education, but must do so when education is funded from the taxation everyone must pay. One extreme view is that taxation represents coercion or theft, as people have no choice about whether to pay it.

Setting the rate

Governments have to find a balance when setting taxes. Tax rates have to be set at a level that will raise enough money to fund a government's spending programme. But if rates are too high it acts as a disincentive to work and therefore reduces the amount of tax revenue collected.

Some economists maintain that if tax rates are kept low, people have an incentive to work more because they get to keep more of the income they earn. When people spend or invest that money, it makes the economy more vigorous, leading to more revenue in taxes later on. There might even be an increase immediately, as people will work longer hours, so pay more tax overall, even though it is at a lower rate.

If tax rates are higher, people see little 'marginal benefit' (increased income per hour or day worked) and therefore might choose to work less, causing tax revenues to fall. Some of the very rich might move abroad, to countries with lower tax rates, if they believe the tax burden is too great.

The Laffer Curve (below) shows how the relationship between the taxation rate and revenue works. The peak of the curve indicates the rate at which most tax is collected. The shape of the curve is disputed, however, and probably varies by time and place. It might be symmetrical, with most tax collected at a tax rate of 50 per cent or less, or it might be asymmetrical. There might even be two peaks. The idea of the curve goes back to 14th-century Tunisia and the Arab proto-sociologist Ibn Khaldun, though it is named after the American economist Arthur Laffer (who made no claim to have invented it).

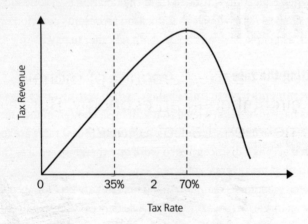

CHAPTER 9

Why don't we just print more money?

There is a fixed amount of money in circulation in an economy. But sometimes it's not enough.

If a nation doesn't have enough money (perhaps it owes a lot in international debt, or its domestic economy is struggling), the question arises: why can't its central bank just print more of it? Then the country could use the newly created money to pay off its debts or invest in, say, building roads, houses and schools. In a way, an economy does this; but it's not quite that straightforward.

Where does money come from?

When the economy is healthy, or 'buoyant', more money is steadily created at a relatively low level by banks making loans. Extra money is not made by printing new bank notes and releasing them into circulation, but by creating bank money with no physical existence. For example, if you took out a mortgage for $200,000, the bank would credit your account with $200,000 and you would owe the bank that amount. Eventually, when you have repaid the debt, the money created for the purposes of the loan disappears again. In the meantime, the bank makes real money from the interest you pay on the loan.

> *'Whenever a bank makes a loan, it simultaneously creates a matching deposit in the borrower's bank account, thereby creating new money.'*
>
> 'Money creation in the modern economy', the Bank of England Quarterly Bulletin

Usually, money is created at a steady rate. Problems arise if banks create too much money and there is so much debt that people and businesses can't afford to pay it back. The banks lose confidence and stop making loans (creating money). The system becomes unbalanced.

Quantitative easing

Regulated creation of new money happens through the activities of the commercial banks, overseen by the central bank. In times of crisis, the central bank can create new money through a process called quantitative easing (QE). It's considered an 'unconventional' monetary policy, so it's only used in exceptional circumstances.

Quantitative easing is not really a licence to print money because no money is actually printed – but it's a licence to create money electronically. If the government feels the country would do better if there were more money in circulation, it creates some and uses it to buy bonds from investors such as insurance companies and pension funds – in this way, the money slips into the regular economy.

There are two effects. Firstly, the interest paid by the bonds decreases. When interest rates are low, there is no incentive to save but plenty of incentive to borrow and spend. Borrowing and spending will reinvigorate the economy as the increase in demand stimulates production. Secondly, financial institutions have more money. Since they have extra, they should be more willing to lend it (responsibly, we hope) to businesses that want to grow, or even to people who want to buy a house or a car or a holiday. The businesses produce more goods and services, which people buy because they now have the money. Because businesses have grown, they employ more people, who then have an income to spend. The whole economy becomes more buoyant. The boost to the economy is supposed to lift it out of recession or stagnation.

Does it work?

Quantitative easing was first tried by the Bank of Japan in the 1990s. Economists are divided about whether or not it worked.

THE FIRST TRILLION

The Bank of England was formed in 1694. It took more than 300 years of moderate lending for banks to amass the first trillion pounds ($1.5 trillion). But it took only eight years to create the next trillion.

The USA has been the most enthusiastic quantitative easer. Between late 2008 and the start of 2015, the Federal Reserve Bank spent $3.7 trillion (£2.4 trillion) on bonds. It claimed success in reducing unemployment and reaching its target rate of inflation (though it is still very low). Between March and November 2009, the Bank of England bought £200 billion ($300 billion) worth of bonds; the economic output of the UK increased by 1.5–2 per cent, which the bank claimed was at least in part a result of QE.

So much for the figures. What do they mean for people? QE invigorates the financial markets rather than the main consumer economy. Stockholders benefit first. In the UK, QE boosted share prices by around 20 per cent. As 40 per cent of shares are owned by the richest 5 per cent of the population, the wealthy benefited the most – to the tune of around £128,000 ($196,000) each. The rest of the population benefits through 'trickle down', which relies on the rich spending their (perceived) wealth in ways that boost the economy of the country. It doesn't help much if they buy a yacht from a foreign boat-builder or go abroad on holiday, flying with an airline based in another country. It does help if they spend their money in local restaurants, eating locally grown food, or use it to buy other goods and services sourced, made or provided in their own country. However, they may spend it on other financial products rather than real goods and services, in which case the trickle-down doesn't happen.

Bonds bite back

There is another problem waiting round the corner. Sooner or later, the banks will want to sell those bonds they bought. At that point, unless carefully judged and handled, interest rates might rise and any recovery that QE has spurred could be stifled. When interest rates are low, people will borrow money to buy goods and services and businesses will borrow money to expand – this drives economic activity. When interest rates are high, people don't want to borrow as it costs too much in repayments. They stop buying things, businesses don't borrow to expand and employ people, and the economy becomes less active. It can slump back to where it started.

> **TRICKLE-DOWN THEORY**
>
> A feature of 'Reaganomics' (the economic policy of US president, Ronald Reagan), trickle-down theory states that if corporations and wealthy individuals are not highly taxed, they will invest their extra wealth in purchases and expansion. This will boost the economy, as the benefit will eventually trickle down to people at lower economic levels. The idea is that if a corporation can keep most of its income, it will build more factories, employ more people, produce more products and therefore generate more income. The increased income of workers and shareholders will be spent, boosting other sectors of the economy. One problem is that if there is no confidence in the economy, the extra money will not be spent but hoarded, because no one has the confidence to invest in expansion.

But, why not *really* print more money?

It might seem that one solution to poverty would be to print more money and just give it to all the people who don't have enough. Why can't we do this?

Suppose a country prints more money so that its people can buy more? Before the new money arrives, a mango costs $1. The country has an economy worth $2 billion. It creates another $2 billion and releases this into the economy. Now many more people can afford to buy mangoes – but mango production hasn't increased. All that happens is that the people selling the mangoes can choose who to sell them to.

They do this by putting the price up: competition for goods has increased demand and this leads to increased prices. Soon mangoes cost $2 instead of $1 and the economy is back where it started: it is no richer because it is not producing any more than it was before.

How about creating money to pay off international debt? That won't work either. Internationally, currencies are not all worth the same. Their value relative to one another fluctuates all the time, representing how much each currency is really 'worth'. If a country prints lots of money, the value of its currency goes down, but its debt does not. The debt is not stored or calculated in each country's own currency.

Suppose the imaginary country Utopia had an exchange rate of two Utopian dollars to one US dollar, a debt to the IMF of 5 billion US dollars (or 10 billion Utopian dollars), and a GDP of 10 billion Utopian dollars. Utopia decides to print another 10 billion Utopian dollars to pay off its debt. But now that the supply of its currency has doubled, the value of the currency has halved. A $1 mango costs $2 and the international debt of US$5 billion is equal to 20 billion Utopian dollars.

CHAPTER 10

Don't we still have to make things?

We hear a lot about how we live in a post-industrial age. But how can we get by without manufacturing?

If your bag contains a smart phone, a tablet computer and the electronic key fob for your car, you don't seem very post-industrial. But to economists and sociologists, 'post-industrial' means that the manufacturing sector of the economy has been overtaken by another, non-industrial sector. Today the service sector and knowledge economy are larger than the manufacturing sector in the economies of many countries.

From agriculture to industry

Long ago, most people worked in farming. Until as recently as the second half of the 19th century, nearly three-quarters of the population worked in agriculture, even in developed nations. The means of production are first employed to meet needs, and then to supply wants once needs have been met. Until the 20th century, agriculture was very labour intensive. Today, in richer countries, only 2–3 per cent of the population works in agriculture, freeing up labour for other types of production.

Even with most of the population working in farming, agriculture never accounted for more than about half a country's GDP. It's just not very productive in economic terms as food has to be cheap enough for everyone to afford. In richer countries, agriculture now accounts for only 1–2 per cent of GDP. That's not because we aren't growing as much food – it's because other contributors to GDP have grown massively.

Leaving the farm . . .

Before the invention of agricultural machinery, sowing, weeding, fertilizing and harvesting crops was hard work. As farming became mechanized, people were freed up to do other kinds of work, such as manufacturing. In Britain, the change from agriculture to industry began during the Industrial Revolution of the 18th and 19th centuries, when efficient, mechanized ploughs, seed-drills and hoes took over much manual work. The development of mechanization in manufacturing drew redundant farmworkers into cities to work long hours operating machinery.

In the mid-20th century another burst of mechanization on farms led to a further drop in agricultural work. This was accompanied by a massive growth in manufacturing after the end of World War II, making use of new materials and technologies and serving a newly wealthy and optimistic population. In the 1950s and 1960s, manufacturing was at its height in Western Europe and the USA, employing nearly 40 per cent of the population.

. . . and leaving the factory

As mechanization liberated people from backbreaking jobs on farms, so it later freed them from repetitive jobs in factories. The mechanization of factories enabled producers to make things much more efficiently and required fewer people, at least in the developed world. Now, in most of the richer nations, only around 10 per cent of people work in manufacturing. Exceptions include Taiwan (28 per cent) and Germany (20 per cent).

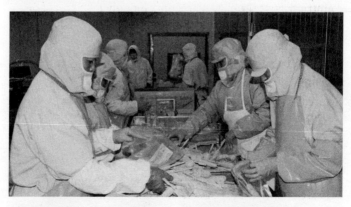

A food processing production line in a factory in northern China.

In the developing economies, manpower is still a cheap manufacturing resource. Many of the goods we buy in developed economies are produced in crowded sweatshops and factories where labour is cheaper than mechanization. Some manufacturing processes are difficult or impossible to mechanize and these, too, are predominantly carried out in areas with a plentiful supply of cheap labour.

Still making things

In the early 1980s, manufacturing was responsible for 57 per cent of world trade; by 1998–2000 it had risen to 78 per cent. In 2009–11 it had fallen again, but was still higher than before at 69 per cent. So manufacturing is still an important economic component, even if fewer people work in it.

With a typical 10 per cent of the population working in manufacturing and 3 per cent in agriculture, a lot of the workforce of a developed country is available for other industries. Many people work in service industries: tourism, education, law, medicine, banking, retail and so on. Service industries don't produce anything new, though they might reconfigure aspects of the economy, by 'adding value' to a cake,

for example, by selling it in a café on a nice plate. Many service industries are, so far, still quite staff-intensive.

> ### THE 1, 2, 3 OF INDUSTRIES
>
> **Primary industries** deal in raw materials: digging metals from the ground, drilling for oil, and so on.
>
> **Secondary industries** process raw materials to make things (manufacturing), turning metal into cars and wheat into bread and cakes, for example.
>
> **Tertiary industries** don't produce any physical products, but provide a service. They move the cars around, sell the cakes in cafés, and provide the bank loan to set up the café.

Is it really a good idea?

In many instances, developed economies have moved a lot of their manufacturing offshore to areas where land and labour are much cheaper. In some instances they don't manufacture at all, but buy things from manufacturers to sell in Western markets. Relatively few clothes or electronic goods, for example, are made in Western Europe or the USA; most are made in Asia, which has become the 'workshop of the world'. The dependence for GDP by Western economies on service industries seemed fine when they were doing well. It even had the aura of being clean and sophisticated. None of those grubby factories or poking around in the dirt for us, thank you; we can live by banking, real estate and insurance.

But can we? The financial crash of 2008 demonstrated how vulnerable a service-based economy is. It's particularly vulnerable when a lot of the services are actually – in most people's terms – illusory: when they involve selling financial 'products' that are barely related to anything in the real world, such as derivatives, futures and reinsurance bundles (see Chapter 21). The global recession did not come about because we no longer grew enough food, made enough cars, nursed enough patients in hospitals or ran enough hotels. All those industries were doing exactly what they had done for years, and remained productive.

SAME JOB, DIFFERENT SECTOR

In recent years, many organizations have begun to outsource functions that are not their main business. An example would be a garment factory which outsources its canteen to a catering company and its cleaning to a cleaning company. When people were employed by the garment factory as chefs or cleaners, their jobs were part of the manufacturing sector. Once they are employed by a catering or cleaning company, they are part of the service sector.

CHAPTER 11

What are you paying for?

Marketing experts work hard to set prices at a level which will encourage people to buy things.

Setting prices sounds as though it should be easy. But there is psychology and sociology involved in getting pricing right. One important factor is whether people feel they have made the right judgement – pressurizing them rarely works.

You can approach this chapter from the point of view of a buyer or a seller. If you are a buyer, it will make you wise to some of the tricks retailers are trying to play on you. If you're a seller, you could try some of the tricks – they work (at least on people who haven't read about them).

Choosing to pay

People's willingness to pay more or less for goods and services depends on personal criteria that vary, but they are combinations of:

- perceived value: does the item deliver features they value?
- utility: how well does the item do what they want it to do?
- quality: is a more expensive item better quality than a cheaper item?
- prestige: will their social standing be enhanced by choosing a more costly item?
- tribal affiliation: is the item a badge of membership to a particular social group?
- availability: is the item more difficult to acquire than a cheaper item?
- trust/risk: do consumers trust the more expensive item to be more reliable or expect the cheaper one to be a risky purchase that might fall short of expectations in some way?
- ethics: is the expensive item more ethically acceptable (low carbon, organic, for example) or sold by a type of organization that consumers want to support (such as a local independent retailer rather than a chain)?

Buy it, it's cheap!

We often see items advertised as cheaper than competitors' products. In many markets, you'd expect that to be a persuasive argument – after all, one tin of tomatoes is much the same as another, especially if they're the same brand from a different shop – but it can make people suspicious. If a retailer points out that one product is cheaper than another, customers may suspect that the cheap product is not as good. They start to feel they might be being tricked, or coerced, neither of which they like. They might buy the more expensive option to avoid being cheated or because buying the cheaper one makes them seem penny-pinching or impoverished.

People will buy if they think something is a bargain – that is, cheaper than its true value. If an item is advertised as sale price or reduced, caution disappears. A study at MIT and the University of Chicago revealed that people were more likely to buy a product if it was marked down from $48 to $40 than if it was full price at $39.

As shoppers, we have little to go on when trying to determine the value of something; there is an imbalance of information, with the sellers knowing far more about their products than we do.

NET ECONOMIC GAIN

The value a consumer gains by paying less than they were willing to is known as net economic gain. Assume apples and pears both cost $3 a kilo. You prefer apples and would be willing to pay $4 a kilo for them. For pears, you would only be willing to pay $3.20 a kilo.

If you buy a kilo of each for $3, you make $1 net economic gain from the apples (as you have saved the $1 you would have been willing to pay), but you only make a 20 cents net economic gain from the pears.

Confidence tricks

One appeal of internet auction sites such as eBay is that we can see how much people value something, and we take a cue from them. Most people are rather insecure about their own ability to judge value. This leads to caution, particularly where there is an imbalance of information between buyer and seller. Someone buying a second-hand car, for example, has much less information about the car they are looking at than the seller has. Consequently they are likely to be wary, fearing it might have hidden faults, and will be prepared to pay less than if they had confidence in it.

Why do people pay more than they have to?

At the opposite end of the scale there are those who knowingly pay more than they need to for items. Paying more can often secure better quality, or an item with more features, or better sales and after-sales service. People might buy a well-known brand because they have more faith in it – it's a way of reducing the risk of purchasing. But some purchasing decisions go beyond quality and trust.

While a $5 T-shirt may not last as long as a $50 T-shirt, a $500 T-shirt probably won't be any better quality than the $50 one. You can buy an excellent watch for $500, yet people buy watches that cost $10,000 and more. Adding gold and diamonds to a watch doesn't make it better at keeping the time. So why buy it? People value aesthetic design and are willing to pay more for things that look good, but not usually to the tune of an extra $9,500. At this point, people are paying for social value: what they think the item says to others about them.

Prestige and tribal affiliation

Expensive items are like a badge of membership to a social group. Again this can be associated with trust and risk, particularly if people trust the judgement of the group they identify with a product, while knowing little about the product and alternatives. Tribal affiliation explains why so many people buy an iPhone without comparing it with other phones on the market, and why there are trends in everything from clothing brands to holiday destinations.

CONTEXT IS ALL

Researchers from Stanford and Rice universities offered two identical CDs on eBay with starting bids of $1.99. One listing was flanked by the same CD, auctioned with a starting bid of $0.99, and the other was flanked by the same CD starting at $5.99. The researchers found that the CD flanked by more expensive copies always received more bids and sold for a higher price than the CD flanked by cheaper copies. People's perception of the value of the CD was influenced by the other offers.

Then the researchers repeated the test, but this time added text pointing out the price difference, and suggested that customers compare the prices. Bidding patterns changed. People waited longer to bid, and the price of the adjacent CDs made no difference to what they were willing to pay. Once the choice to compare was not theirs, they were distrustful and less interested.

If we don't research the possibilities, if we're insecure about our taste or social position, we'll buy what others are buying if they are people we identify with or aspire to be like. Advertisers cash in on this by showing models using a product in settings that are more glamorous or exotic than those of their target audience. The idea is to make you feel that you, too, will be one of the rich/trendy/attractive/young people if you own this product. You won't – you'll be the same person, with a product for which you have probably paid over the odds.

Buy it, we don't want you to!

Most of us have experienced being looked down on by snooty shop assistants. We either brazen it out or leave. 'Don't they want me to buy anything?' we grumble internally. Well, no, they don't. If you're not the kind of customer they like to think patronizes the shop, they'll feel your presence will diminish their brand. For some people, being treated in this disrespectful way doesn't deter them. The antipathy of the shop staff adds to the appeal of the product, making it more desirable. This type of customer is the aspirational purchaser, someone who buys because he or she wants to be like the people who possess those goods.

The four 'Ps'

Research at the Marshall Business School in California suggests consumers can be divided into four groups according to their attitude to luxury brands. These are: patricians (old money), parvenus (new money), poseurs (less money) and proletarians (not much money).

Patricians buy luxury goods because they want the quality and because they are loyal to the brand. They are not interested in flashing the label to the general public and will generally pick the non-ostentatious designs that will only be recognized by other patricians.

Parvenus do want to flash the label, as they need to signal to other wealthy people that they are one of the tribe. They're the people who buy Louis Vuitton luggage with the conspicuous logo, the Gucci sunglasses with the prominent Gucci badge, the flashy red Ferrari sports car and the distinctive red-soled Louboutin shoes.

Poseurs want to flash the brand, but can't always afford to do that. They're in the market for cheap lookalike brands and imported fakes that the patricians and parvenus wouldn't touch with a bargepole.

Proletarians don't care about image and just buy what they like and can afford.

The result is that luxury brands such as Gucci and Louis Vuitton often have two types of product – one that is ostentatious and sells to the parvenus and one that is discreet, more expensive, and sells to the patricians. The cheaper, lookalike and 'knock-off' products are predominantly of the parvenu-targeted designs, because that's who the poseurs are emulating.

BUY IT, IT'S EXPENSIVE!

Business psychologist Robert Cialdini cites a jeweller whose turquoise jewellery wasn't selling. She had intended to mark it down to half price, but accidentally marked it as double the price. Suddenly, seeing that turquoise jewellery was expensive, people assumed it was special and bought it.

Wealth ⟶		
Desire for status ↓	Proletarians	Patricians
	Poseurs	Parvenus

SILLY MONEY

Who would buy the following?

- a gold iPhone for $100,000 (£65,000)
- a gold-and-diamond Bluetooth headset for $50,000 (£32,500)
- Gold staples (yes, staples for paper) for $175 (£113) a packet, though you can get them for $59 (£38) if you shop around
- a crocodile-skin umbrella for $50,000 (£32,500)
- diamond-encrusted contact lenses for $15,000 (£9,700)

Answer – parvenus!

CHAPTER 12

Why can't I get a job?

Unemployment rates rise
and fall – but why?

The traditional pattern of working life used to be that a person started work at perhaps the age of 16, 18 or 21, depending on how long they stayed in education, and carried on for 40–50 years, then retired. But this pattern has become less common. People now have periods of unemployment, give up paid work to look after young children or older relatives, retire early (or late), retrain, go back to studying or, in some cases, never work at all.

The need for labour

Labour is one of the factors of production along with land and capital. Without labour, nothing is produced or sold. Even if we imagine a completely automated factory making goods, there will still be people who maintain and repair the machinery, deal with orders and the purchase of raw materials, market the goods and, perhaps at a different company, make the machines that make the goods.

The labour market

There is a market for labour, just as there is a market for goods and services and for the other aspects of production. It follows the familiar pattern of supply and demand curves (see Chapter 3). When there is a demand for labour and not enough workers, wages rise. When there are more people looking for work than there is suitable work for them, wages fall.

Labour is closely tied to human capital – the skills and abilities of people that have been developed through training, education and experience.

Interchangeable jobs and workers

Some types of job demand few skills or personal qualities, so most people would be capable of doing them. For example, cleaning a cinema between showings of films is a job almost any person with normal mobility and vision could do. This means a huge proportion of the population could do it, though not all will want to.

There are also many jobs that don't require skills and training. Let's suppose a person with no training wants an unskilled job and there are two jobs available with the same rate of pay: one is picking fruit on a farm; the other is picking up litter in a cinema. The person might apply to the cinema because they will get to see some movies, and perhaps the hours fit better with their other commitments (such as looking after children). Or they might apply to the farm because they prefer to work outdoors. If either the cinema or farm finds it cannot attract workers, it might decide to increase the wages on offer. Then applicants have to decide which is more important to them: better pay or being outside/seeing movies?

Too few workers: demand for labour

In a market where there are fewer workers willing to do a job, employers are forced to offer incentives to attract staff. These might include more pay, more flexible working hours, or extra benefits (free fruit from the farm, perhaps). The demand for labour in any industry is affected by:

- the price of other factors of production: if the price of automation drops, workers will be replaced by machines
- increasing efficiency: if working practices become more productive, fewer workers are needed
- demand for goods: if demand rises, the demand for labour increases in order to raise supply

The labour market, like any other, follows the rules of supply and demand. Extra incentives attract new workers to the market. Perhaps higher wages mean that people can afford

childcare or transport, enabling them to take a job, or older
people delay retirement so they can earn more. As more people
enter the market, the supply of workers rises, so the higher
demand is met. Wages don't need to rise any further because,
if they did, people in skilled jobs might decide to take a more
boring job in exchange for better pay, so the pool of workers
would grow quickly.

Markets are linked: if the wage a cinema has to pay cleaners
is too high, the price of cinema tickets will have to rise to
cover the cost. Then fewer people will go to the cinema, fewer
cleaners will be needed, and wages will fall again.

Too many workers: supply of labour

Suppose there are too many workers and too few unskilled
jobs available. The supply of labour is affected by:

- population change: a rise in the birthrate will lead to
  a later bulge in the working population. A fall in the
  birthrate will lead to fewer workers being available
  later on.
- migration: if workers move from one area to another to
  find work, more labour will be available and wages will
  probably fall.

- tax rates: these affect the marginal benefits of working. People might not want to work extra hours if the tax arrangements mean they will gain little or no extra cash for their efforts.

When the supply of labour is high, employers don't need to provide extra incentives. They can offer low wages and still fill the vacancies. The level to which wages can drop depends on the situation in any particular country and whether the government intervenes in the labour market. Some countries have a legal minimum wage and all employers must pay at least this amount. Some have a welfare system that will support people who are out of work, or top up the earnings of people in low-paid jobs. Generous welfare support means that people might choose not to work for a low wage if they can get as much from state benefits.

If government provides subsidies for people in low-paid work, the employer can get away with paying low wages in the knowledge that the state will top up the workers' income. If there is no regulation and no welfare back-up, employers can get away with paying very low wages and forcing people to work very long hours. Most developed economies have introduced legislation setting out minimum pay and conditions to try to prevent the exploitation of workers, but some businesses get round this by outsourcing to places where no such laws apply (or where they are not enforced).

Scarcity: skills shortage

High unemployment does not always mean it is difficult to find work. Even during an economic downturn, some skills may be in high demand. Despite high unemployment in many economies, employers sometimes grumble that they can't find the staff they need. This often applies to people with specialist skills such as engineers or surgeons. These jobs command high wages because they are difficult to do and employees have invested time, effort and, perhaps, money learning to do them. They want to be rewarded for their investment by earning more than an unskilled worker. It is not a simple matter for an unemployed person to retrain as an engineer or a surgeon, so the high demand does not rapidly lead to an increase in supply.

Other factors

The labour market is complicated by factors other than money. A person with a burning ambition to become a vet is unlikely to train in accountancy just because there are more jobs for accountants. A person who wants to be a musician, but has the qualifications to become an engineer, might still choose to be a musician and earn less than she could as an engineer. She might even take an unskilled job to support herself while trying to carve out a career in music. The personal satisfaction she gains from being a musician is more important to her than money or job security.

Another problem is that the school or college system in a particular country might not produce potential candidates with the qualifications or skills which employers demand. Employers may therefore feel the need to train new recruits themselves, which is both costly and time-consuming. There might, for example, be low levels of IT-literacy among school-leavers, or more people with management qualifications than there are management vacancies, but fewer with the foreign-language skills needed for international trade. People who can speak Chinese or Arabic may be in short supply, in which case an English-speaker who can conduct business negotiations in one of these languages will be in more demand than a monoglot English speaker.

People need to live

Workers have additional needs, such as affordable accommodation, schooling for their children, reliable transport to work, and so on; these have an impact on the labour market. For example, high housing costs can force both skilled and unskilled workers to move away from an area. In this case, wages will have to rise, and/or housing and transport costs will have to fall to avoid a labour shortage. For many cities around the world, this is already a major issue. Governments must decide whether to intervene and, for example, provide low-cost social housing, subsidized public transport and increased provision for schooling and healthcare to draw workers back to the cities.

Mobility of labour

The labour market is also affected by the mobility of the potential workforce. This has two aspects: geographical mobility and occupational mobility.

Geographical mobility describes people who are willing and able to move in order to take work. This is the type of mobility demonstrated by the large number of Eastern European workers who moved to Western Europe following the fall of the Soviet Union. As plumbers, electricians and other skilled workers moved west, they easily found employment because they were willing to work longer hours and for lower wages than Western workers in the same trades.

Occupational mobility describes people's willingness and ability to change professions – from hairdresser to swimming instructor, for instance. Within the unskilled and semi-skilled labour market, this is relatively easy. For skilled jobs, it is difficult, time-consuming and costly because the necessary skills take longer to acquire. Workers might not be willing or able to retrain for a different type of job.

Government intervention

Direct government intervention and changes to legislation can affect the job market.

If a government sets a minimum wage, the short-term effect may be that job vacancies fall and unemployment rises. But experience in Europe suggests that, in the longer term, a minimum wage can increase the demand for labour. A higher wage means employers and workers are investing more in the job, and productivity increases as a result.

Legislation which gives employers more costs or responsibilities – such as a company pension – might result in staff cutbacks. If the government offers subsidies to employers, perhaps to take on school leavers or people with disabilities, this might lead to more jobs for certain groups of workers. Similarly, if government relaxes regulations over pay and conditions or reduces the financial burden of employing people, demand for labour is likely to rise.

The labour market is also affected by anti-discrimination laws, which increase the number of available workers, by subsidized childcare (making more parents available for work), and by encouraging or subsidizing training schemes. Relaxing or tightening controls on immigration can affect the labour market, as it increases or reduces the number of foreign workers available to employers.

CHAPTER 13

What should the state own?

In some countries, the state owns vital utilities, industries and infrastructure; in other countries, they are in private hands.

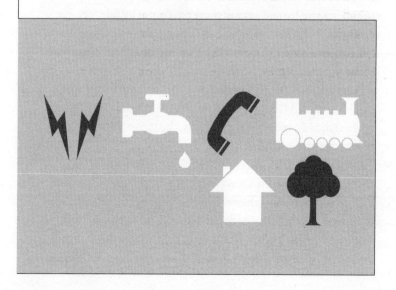

All governments accept that some goods and services are essential. These include clean drinking water, gas and electricity, military defence, a police and judicial system, and so on. But governments take different views on how they should be provided. Should they be state owned or privately owned? Should they be run as a monopoly, with fixed prices, or should free-market forces determine the costs? In some countries with free-market economies, utilities such as gas and electricity are state owned, whereas in other countries they are privately owned. Such decisions tend to be made on political as much as economic grounds.

Types of good

Economists distinguish between public goods and private goods. Confusingly, 'goods' in this case is not the same as 'goods' that are distinct from services; this time, goods include services and are anything that brings benefit to someone.

Private goods are those that are limited in supply and from which people can be excluded. If something is limited in supply, its use by one person prevents its use by another. For example, if I buy a pizza and eat it, it's gone for good and no one else can have it. This makes it a rivalrous good: people are rivals in consumption.

Private goods are also excludable: this means that people can be excluded from using them. People can only go to the cinema to see a movie if they pay for the ticket. Without a ticket, they are excluded.

Public goods are non-rivalrous and non-excludable. This means that use by one person doesn't prevent use by another, and people can't be excluded from benefiting from it. Examples include street lighting, national defence and firework displays. The fact that one person is able to make use of street lighting or enjoy a firework display doesn't prevent others from doing so. Similarly, no one can be excluded from the benefits of national defence, street lighting or seeing fireworks. Not only can people not be excluded – they often can't choose to exclude themselves. Many public goods are non-refusable. People can't individually refuse a national space programme or fluoride added to drinking water.

Semi- or quasi-public goods have some elements of private goods, so may be excludable. Use of a library is excludable: people without a library card are not allowed to borrow books, even though the library may be funded by taxes and the card issued without any charge. But the library is non-rivalrous – one person using the library doesn't stop another using it. Some goods are semi-public because they can become rivalrous. For example, a road network can be semi-public if there are tolls on certain bridges or roads, and a beach can be semi-public if at peak times it is so busy that there is no space for more visitors.

Free-riders

Many goods that a state needs to provide are either public or semi-public. Non-excludable goods present a problem for the state as they can't be provided exclusively to the people who pay for them, and withheld from others. This leads to the problem of free-riders: people who benefit from a service, but don't contribute to its cost.

Imagine a country, Neutopia, that wants a free-market economy. The government believes people should choose how to spend their money. Few of Neutopia's citizens want to contribute to paying for sewers, an army, a police force and street lighting. They would probably not even want to pay to have a government. Most citizens just want to enjoy themselves – taking holidays, enjoying evenings out and owning fast cars. As they have limited financial resources, if they had to choose between paying for military equipment for the army and buying a new car for themselves, most would buy a car. They soon realize that the goods they don't want to pay for are non-excludable; all citizens benefit from public services, even if they don't pay for them.

When a state has too many free-riders, it causes problems. With no money to pay for public services, the infrastructure will begin to collapse and criminals will take advantage of the absence of a police force. There is no guarantee that the free market will invest adequately in public services, or have the means to maintain them to an adequate standard. Therefore governments recognize that – however strong their commitment to free-market principles – there are some things the public must pay for whether they like it or not. The way that governments get people to pay for public services is through taxation (see Chapter 8).

Semi-public services, such as swimming pools and sports centres, are expensive to build and maintain. But for those people who cannot afford the membership fees of private sports clubs, the health benefits are enormous.

Merit goods

Some public goods and some private goods are also classed as merit goods. These are good for society as a whole. They include education, healthcare, sports facilities, museums, libraries and public broadcasting. If merit goods were left entirely to the free market, there is no guarantee that private companies would provide sufficient facilities for all who need them at a price they can afford. As the facilities benefit the whole of society, most governments choose to provide at least some of them free or cheaply at the point of use.

It might seem that the person who benefits from education or vaccination is the person who is educated or vaccinated. In fact the whole of society benefits from having a better-educated population as it leads generally to more productive workers which, in turn, trigger economic growth. Similarly, if most of the population is vaccinated it reduces the risk of infectious diseases spreading, and the whole of society benefits from herd immunity.

Demerit goods

The opposite of merit goods are demerit goods. These are over-provided by the market and harmful to society. Examples are street drugs, alcohol and tobacco products. Governments can intervene in several ways. They can ban the demerit goods (as they do with street drugs); they can use taxes to increase the price of the goods and thus reduce consumption (as with tobacco and alcohol); and they can use education and campaigns to discourage people from buying and using them.

Paying for things you don't want

There are several reasons a government might decide to make people pay for something they would not personally choose to pay for, and different ways of doing it. For example, people might be forced or persuaded to pay for education (for their own children or others), for car insurance, health insurance and into a pension fund.

Governments can use taxation or legislation to ensure that people pay. It's a legal requirement to take out car insurance if you want to drive on the roads, for example, to guarantee that you can compensate other road users if you have an accident and injure them or damage their car. It might be a legal requirement to pay into a fund for a pension or health insurance, or the money might be taken from your income. A government might use advertising and public information campaigns to try to persuade people to pay into a pension fund, or make vaccination a legal requirement for children before they can register at a school.

Who does the work?

Once a local or national government body has decided which public goods and services to fund, it must choose how to provide them. It can employ staff itself or contract out to private firms to provide the service. It is not economic for a government to keep all the staff it may ever need permanently on its books. Local authorities do not employ people to repair roads, for example. Instead they pay a private company to do this as and when required. At the opposite end of the scale, schools need a certain number of teachers on a permanent basis, so teachers will be directly employed by the local authority all year round.

Should we privatize essential industries?

Views on how many and what type of services should be provided by the state vary and, as governments change, so does state provision. The more an economy tends towards a free market, the more essential services will be privately owned. Some that were previously state owned might be sold to private investors. The UK government has sold off many state-owned services in the past 50 years, including British Gas, British Telecom, the Post Office and British Rail. The argument put forward to justify privatization is that services will be run more efficiently and competitively in the private sector and this will benefit consumers. In fact, many of the privatized services in the UK are now largely owned by state-run enterprises based overseas, which have bought up shares

Advantages of privatization	Disadvantages of privatization
Improved efficiency as private firms seek to maximize profit by cutting costs.	Fall in standards as economic considerations are put ahead of quality of service.
Ability to take a long-term view: those in charge are not restricted to an elected term in office.	The wishes of shareholders may take precedence over the needs of employees, the business itself and consumers of the service. For example, shareholders hope for high dividends (pay-outs on their shares), and might vote for this instead of buying new trains or pipelines that would improve the service in the long term.
Increased competition benefits consumers if it leads to falling prices and rising standards.	In the case of natural monopolies, such as water companies, lack of competition and state regulation can lead to consumer exploitation (such as higher prices but poorer service) as consumers have no alternative.
Lack of political interference; a state-run organization might be reluctant to cut staff, for instance, because of the political repercussions.	Can lead to fragmentation, with some areas of responsibility or parts of the market being overlooked or neglected.
The sale of shares in the organization raises funds for the state.	It is a one-off injection of cash, and the state benefits little (only in taxes) from any profit the organization makes later.

on the open market. Much of the profit these businesses make goes overseas to state-run organizations or to shareholders, so is not reinvested for the benefit of UK consumers.

Whereas right-leaning governments tend to favour privatization, left-leaning governments are likely to bring more services into state or public ownership and might even re-nationalize industries sold to the private sector. One example is the UK rail network infrastructure (such as tracks, stations and signals), which was privately owned, then brought into public ownership, then privatized again, and has since been re-nationalized. Neither private nor public ownership has proved more efficient.

Many economists feel that privatization is a valid option for industries in which there is no natural monopoly and where free-market competition will ensure that prices are kept down and standards kept high. Telecoms is an example of a service that can be provided by many alternative suppliers in a competitive market with few adverse effects on the service. Water supply is a natural monopoly, however. There is no opportunity for consumer choice, so no market-driven incentive for suppliers to lower prices or raise standards.

CHAPTER 14

Is inflation good or bad?

No shopper likes rising prices.
But price stagnation is
bad for the economy.

Inflation is a sustained rise in prices over time; it reduces the purchasing power of money. It means that a dollar, pound or euro will buy less today than it did last year. For example, if you have $1 and a chocolate bar costs $0.99, you can buy one. If inflation pushes the price up to $1.01, that chocolate bar has become unaffordable.

A basket of good(ie)s

Inflation is measured within an economy, showing how prices change over time. As the price of individual items is affected by many factors, inflation is measured by tracking the price of a selection of goods and services that households typically buy. These goods are called a basket, market basket or consumer bundle. The basket represents the type of things the average person is likely to buy. In the UK, popular staples and essentials such as bacon, tea, bread, milk and petrol have been included in the basket right from the start. Items are chosen to reflect their importance in people's spending patterns at any given moment. But these change over time, so particular goods and services may be added to or dropped from the consumer basket as fashions (or purchasing patterns) alter. In 2015, for instance, yoghurt drinks and sat navs were dropped. Sweet potatoes and subscriptions to streaming music channels (Spotify, for example) were added to the basket.

This represents the declining popularity of yoghurt drinks and sat navs and the increasing popularity of sweet potatoes and Spotify. The basket also includes typical amounts for utility bills; transport costs, such as rail season tickets; entertainments such as cable TV subscriptions and cinema tickets; childminding and care-home costs; one-off large purchases, such as holidays, cars and fridges, and so on. When the UK basket was introduced in 1947, it contained 150 items; by 2015, the number had risen to more than 700.

Consumer price index

We can tell whether prices are rising or falling by monitoring the changing price of the basket. This is known as the consumer price index (CPI). Imagine that in one year the price of goods in the basket was €300. We will call this Year 0. The following year (Year 1) the price was €330, and the year after (Year 2) it was €390.

To calculate CPI, we need a base year; let's take Year 0 as the base. CPI is calculated as:

So for the base year (Year 0):

$$\frac{\text{Cost in current year}}{\text{Cost in base year}} \times 100 \qquad \frac{£300}{£300} \times 100 = 100$$

For the next year (Year 1):

And for the following year (Year 2):

$$\frac{£330}{£300} \times 100 = 110 \qquad \frac{£390}{£300} \times 100 = 130$$

The CPI is 100, 110 and 130 respectively. The inflation rate is calculated from the difference in CPI between two years, so the inflation rate over the first year (Year 0 to Year 1) is 110 – 100 = 10 per cent. The inflation rate over the next year (Year 1 to Year 2) is 130 – 110 = 20 per cent.

This nation is heading for bad times

Like any tool, the CPI has its limitations. For one thing, it fails to take account of the intelligence and autonomy of consumers who will adjust their purchasing as prices change. If apples become very expensive, consumers will buy fewer apples and more of another fruit. If breakfast cereal becomes very cheap, consumers might buy more of that and fewer croissants. This is called substitution bias; people will seek to cut their

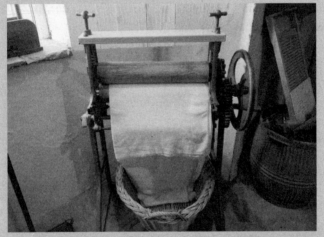
expenditure by substituting one item for another. Changes in the quality of goods and services are also not reflected. For example, if technological changes improve the quality of an item in the basket, but the price stays the same, this benefits the consumer. The CPI does not reflect this, however.

Why do prices go up?

Economists often focus on two causes of inflation: cost-push and demand-pull.

Cost-push inflation occurs when the costs associated with production rise (wages, taxes, cost of imports and raw materials). As the cost of manufacturing or supplying a service rises, the price of the product must also go up if the business is to continue making a profit. So rising costs push up prices.

Demand-pull inflation happens when there is more demand for goods and services than can be met by the available supply. Producers can then demand a higher price and, being opportunistic, they do so. This happens when an economy is growing, people have more money to spend, and their demands can't be met by supply.

Bad effects

It's easy to see why people don't like inflation. Goods cost more; the same amount of money buys us less. Life is not as much fun when you can't afford things. On the whole, though, wages rise with inflation, so the effect is marginal unless inflation is either unexpected or gets out of hand.

THE HEMLINE INDEX

Economists have found correlations between particular products or choices and consumer confidence. People feel they can afford a small luxury when they are confident their income won't fall. In 1926, economist George Taylor introduced the Hemline Index, which plotted the length of women's skirts against stock prices. In buoyant economies, such as those of the 1920s and 1960s, hemlines tend to rise. In poorer economic climates, such as those of the 1930s and early 1990s, hemlines tend to drop. Short hairstyles are also a sign of prosperity because they cost more to maintain.

The people who suffer most when inflation hits are those living on a fixed income or on savings. The value of savings is eroded by inflation because the same amount of saved money buys less.

Going down . . .

In general, inflation is a sign of a flourishing economy: demand-pull inflation suggests that people are prosperous. During the recent years of economic turmoil, inflation has been low, even non-existent. The opposite of inflation is deflation – it happens when prices fall.

That sounds like a benefit as it means we can buy more stuff for the same money. But economists and politicians don't like deflation. It is generally caused by a drop in the supply of money or credit, meaning that people can't afford to buy so much. As a result, prices drop to entice people to spend more. Deflation can lead or contribute to recession or depression. As buying stalls and prices drop, profits on the sales that are made also fall, and businesses might have to lay off staff and cut back on production. Higher unemployment means people have even less money to spend, so demand drops further. The economy falls into a vicious circle of decreasing demand, which leads to lower prices, lower profits, lower employment, and to a further decrease in demand and spending.

A period of deflation occurred in Japan in the early 1990s. The Japanese government dropped interest rates to zero to try to boost spending, but this did not have the desired rapid effect. It took until 2006 for the Japanese economy to start to recover. Europe and the USA tried to avoid deflation in the 2010s through quantitative easing – producing more money to release into the economy to boost spending (see Chapter 9).

Too much money

Too much inflation can be worse than too little.

Hyperinflation occurs when prices rise out of all control. The most famous historical example of hyperinflation occurred in the German Weimar Republic between 1921 and 1924. Germany had financed World War I with debt, and as a

THE WORST OF BOTH WORLDS

Stagflation is a portmanteau word built from *stagnation* and *inflation*. The stagnation of the market means there is little economic growth and there is steadily high unemployment. At the same time, inflation is high. It's not a good economic environment. With high unemployment and no growth, income doesn't keep pace with prices so the standard of living drops.

Stagflation happened in the 1970s in the developed world when an oil crisis started in the Middle East and pushed the price of fuel up. This meant that the prices of most goods also rose as the cost of products made from oil increased, as did the price of all forms of transport used to move the products, and that of heating and electricity generation. As price rises were not accompanied by economic growth, wages did not rise in line with inflation and people became poorer. The 1970s stagflation continued as the central banks overstimulated the money supply, causing a price/wage spiral.

consequence the international value of its currency had fallen from 4.2 marks to the US dollar at the start of the war, to 32 marks to the US dollar at the end of 1919. Crippled by the need to pay reparations for World War I in gold or foreign currency, Germany needed to purchase foreign money at any cost, so printed more and more marks in order to do so. The result was that the value of the mark fell even further – to 330 marks/US dollar by the end of 1921.

In 1922, conferences held to deal with the war reparations crisis failed, and the mark went into freefall and hyperinflation. By December 1922, the exchange rate was 800 marks/US dollar; just eleven months later this rose to more than 4.2 trillion marks/US dollar. The wholesale price index (1 in the base year of 1914) was 726 billion by November 1923. Notes were printed in denominations of hundreds of millions, billions, and finally trillions of marks; the largest denomination note printed was 100 trillion marks. By the end of the crisis, in late 1923, 300 paper mills and 150 printing companies using 2,000 presses worked day and night to print currency.

The effect on the German people was catastrophic. Any money held before hyperinflation was worthless – the price of a house would not buy a loaf of bread. As soon as people realized that their money was losing value, they started to spend it rapidly. This drove prices up further, increasing the rate of inflation. To start with, the wealthy moved their money into art, gold, jewellery and real estate, but then ordinary people bought things – *any* things. An alternative economy based on barter grew up. It was a practical necessity because in money, in November 1923, a loaf of bread cost 200 billion marks and an egg cost 80 billion. This was 500 billion times the cost of these goods in 1914.

> *'At 11:00 in the morning a siren sounded, and everybody gathered in the factory forecourt, where a five-ton lorry was drawn up loaded brimful with paper money. The chief cashier and his assistants climbed up on top. They read out names and just threw out bundles of notes. As soon as you had caught one you made a dash for the nearest shop and bought just anything that was going.'*
>
> Willy Derkow, a German student in 1923

Not worth the paper it's printed on

As the situation deteriorated, the German people had to move their money about in wheelbarrows. Now worthless banknotes were used as wallpaper or given to children to cut up as craft paper, as they were worth less than real toys. Photos show people burning bundles of notes in stoves (see below), as paper money was of less value than firewood.

Workers were paid in cash at the start of the day and given half an hour in which to spend their wages before they became worthless. Some workers were paid three times a day; they immediately passed money to relatives waiting at the factory gates who took it away to spend. The price of a cup of coffee doubled in the time it took to drink it. Waiters stood on tables and announced revised prices for the menu every half hour.

Fixed

The situation was finally resolved in November 1923 by the introduction of a new currency, the Rentenmark. As there was no gold to back the currency, it was backed by land used for agriculture and business. The land was mortgaged to the tune of 3.2 billion marks in 1913, so 3.2 billion Rentenmark were issued. The value of one Rentenmark was 4.2 US dollars (the value the mark had been before World War I). The new currency was exchanged at the rate of one Rentenmark to one trillion old marks.

Worse than very bad

German hyperinflation was very bad, but the experience of Zimbabwe was even worse. The Zimbabwean dollar, introduced in 1980, underwent three official redenominations; by the end, one fourth-generation dollar was worth 10^{25} first generation dollars (that's a '1' followed by 25 zeros). In April 2009, the Zimbabwean currency was officially abandoned and all transactions in Zimbabwe were carried out in foreign currencies, including the US dollar, South African rand, pound sterling, euro, rupee and Chinese yuan.

Setting the price of porridge

As too much inflation and too little inflation are both a sign of an unhealthy economy, governments aim at a 'Goldilocks zone' of just the right amount of inflation. This is generally considered to be around 2–3 per cent. It allows controlled growth of the economy, without prices outstripping wages, and enough demand to keep suppliers extending their output.

CHAPTER 15

If we are the 99 per cent, who are the 1 per cent?

Inequality is the plague of modern economies.

People are wary of talking about inequality. We can tackle poverty by giving money to charity – even a little bit helps. But to tackle inequality, some of us have to recognize that we have too much compared with people who have too little, and most of us feel uncomfortable thinking about that.

Economists consider inequality in three ways:

- difference in income
- difference in wealth
- difference in consumption

The growing gap

In the 1970s, the top 1 per cent of the US population accounted for around 10 per cent of the national income. Now they account for more than 20 per cent of the national income. But the very top 0.1 per cent of the population has increased its share to 8 per cent of the income – almost as much as the top 1 per cent held 40 years previously.

In 2005, the wealth of Warren Buffet and Bill Gates was equivalent to the wealth of the bottom 40 per cent of the US population (120 million people). It's not only a problem in the USA. The effect is most marked in the capitalist countries that are closest to a free-market model. The UK is approaching the USA in wealth inequality. According to figures released by Oxfam in 2014, 1 per cent of the world's population owns 46 per cent of the wealth, and the richest 85 individuals own as much as the poorest half of the world's population (3.5 billion people).

Now you see it . . .

In 2007, Americans already saw their country as divided into the haves and the have-nots. In 2014, a survey asked US citizens what they thought the relationship between bosses' pay and employees' pay was – and what it should be. On average, people thought it was about 30:1 and should be around 8:1, but some estimates for the ratio were as high as 354:1. On average, a CEO's pay was around $12 million (£7.8m) and an employee's pay around $34,000 (£22,000). In the 1960s, the typical American CEO earned around 20 times as much as the average employee, so by 2014 the ratio had increased by a factor of 17.

The situation is not as bad elsewhere but neither is it healthy, as shown by the table below:

	Actual ratio	What people think it is	What people think it should be
Poland	28:1	13.3	5
Denmark	48:1	3.7	2
Japan	67:1	10	6
Israel	76:1	7	3.6
UK	84:1	13.5	5.3
Australia	93:1	40	8.3
France	104:1	24.2	6.7
Spain	127:1	6.7	3
Germany	147:1	16.7	6.3
Switzerland	148:1	12.3	5
USA	354:1	29.6	6.7

Drawing inequality

The Lorenz curve (see page 142) plots cumulative percentage of the population against cumulative percentage of income or wealth. This means that at the left-hand side, a tiny percentage of the population has earned a tiny percentage of the income,

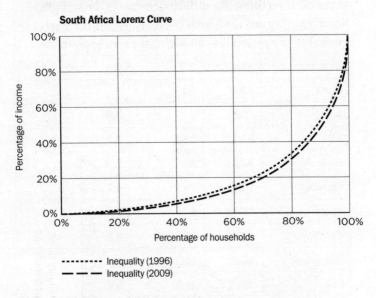

South Africa Lorenz Curve

Percentage of income (y-axis): 0%, 20%, 40%, 60%, 80%, 100%

Percentage of households (x-axis): 0%, 20%, 40%, 60%, 80%, 100%

-------- Inequality (1996)
— — — Inequality (2009)

and at the right-hand side all the population has earned all the income. It's easy to see how unequal a society is by reading off the percentage earned or owned by, say, the bottom 10 per cent or top 20 per cent. The graph shows that in 2009 South Africa was a very unequal society; the bottom 20 per cent of households earned less than 5 per cent of the income in the whole country, whereas the top 10 per cent of households earned more than 50 per cent of the income.

Drawing a straight line at 45 degrees from zero people/income to 100 per cent people/income shows how the curve would look in a perfectly equitable society, in which everyone earned the same. Along the straight line, 20 per cent of the people earn 20 per cent of the income, 50 per cent of the people earn 50 per cent of the income and so on – each percentage point of people earns a percentage point of the income.

The Gini coefficient of inequality

In the diagram below, the difference between the straight line of equality and the Lorenz curve represents the level of inequality in a society. By comparing the area beneath the Lorenz curve and the area beneath the straight line, we can get a measure of inequality known as the Gini coefficient. This measure was developed by the Italian economist Corrado Gini in 1912.

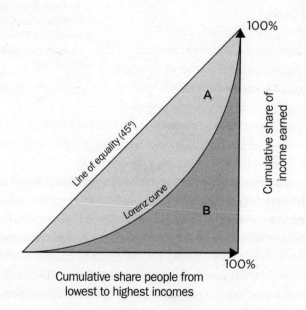

100%

A

Line of equality (45°)

Lorenz curve

B

Cumulative share of income earned

100%

Cumulative share people from lowest to highest incomes

The Gini coefficient is expressed as a number between 0 and 1 (or sometimes between 0 and 100) and shows how the actual Lorenz curve differs from the perfectly equitable position (the straight line graph).

$$G \text{ (gini coefficient)} = A \div (A + B)$$

A Gini coefficient of 0 means an equal economy in which everyone earns or owns the same amount. A coefficient of 1 denotes absolute inequality, where everything is owned or earned by one person.

Who is more and who is less equal?

Using the Gini coefficient as a measure of inequality, the most unequal country in the world was until recently South Africa, with a coefficient of 0.65 in 2011 (World Bank figure). At the same time, China had a Gini coefficient of 0.37 and the USA of about 0.41. Most major economies have a Gini coefficient of between 0.3 and 0.5.

The coefficient differs according to whether it is calculated before or after taking account of taxes and welfare benefits. As these attempt to make society more equal, the coefficient is generally lower if they are taken into account. For example, France's Gini coefficient of 0.485 is reduced to 0.293 after taxes; the UK goes from 0.456 to 0.345, so the UK tax system is not as good at creating equality as the French system.

'We have no paupers. The great mass of our population is of laborers; our rich, who can live without labor, either manual or professional, being few, and of moderate wealth. Most of the laboring class possess property, cultivate their own lands, have families, and from the demand for their labor are enabled to exact from the rich and the competent such prices as enable them to be fed abundantly, clothed above mere decency, to labor moderately and raise their families. Can any condition of society be more desirable than this?'

Thomas Jefferson (1814)

The USA has a pre-tax Gini coefficient almost the same as that of France, at 0.486, but taxation does not reduce it as much: it is still 0.380 after taxes.

How did we get here?

Inequality has become much worse very quickly. Economists cite several reasons for this including: globalization, the increasing use of technology, and neo-liberal politics.

Shanty towns are a stark reminder of the huge gulf between rich and poor.

Globalization has emerged as technology and transport have improved. Corporations are no longer restricted to local or national markets for their goods, but can sell them across the world easily. There is now a global market of around a billion middle-class people with money to spare. With the economies of scale that come from making much larger quantities, manufacturers' production costs are lower per item. They can often make goods more cheaply, too, by building factories close to the source of raw materials and in countries where labour is cheap. Increased profits go to the shareholders, making them richer.

Technology also makes it possible to produce more items with fewer workers. The balance of the means of production shifts from labour to capital. As less is spent on labour and more on buying technology, more money goes to other large corporations and less to individual workers. Again, money accumulates with the owners.

Neo-liberal politics favours the market, so helps business owners more than workers. Recent policies that have contributed to inequality include:

Deregulation: reducing the restrictions on what corporations can do, giving them more freedom to act for profit rather than in the interests of workers, the environment or the population.

Privatization of previously state-owned industries and resources (see Chapter 13): moving ownership and management of these into private hands leads to them generating profit for shareholders rather than benefiting the whole population.

Lower taxes: intended to encourage investment in industry and entrepreneurship. High earners keep more of their income, and spending on public goods is reduced because the government has less tax revenue to spend.

Less protection for unionized workers: there is more freedom in the market if workers can't distort it through grouping together to make demands, such as higher wages or better working conditions.

Finally, a cultural shift has made us more tolerant of wide disparities in income. As the gap between rich and poor has widened, it has also been normalized.

Is it really a problem?

The very wealthy often defend their situation by saying that they generate wealth so should be entitled to the lion's share of the profits they make. Some say they should not be obliged to pay taxes, because wealth generation itself benefits society and many wealthy people aid the poor through charitable donations (referring to the tradition of philanthropy among many wealthy Americans). Morality and entitlement are certainly worth debating, but a more objective point is that high levels of inequality are destabilizing and can't be sustained in the long term. Many economic arguments suggest that capitalism will undermine itself if allowed to create unchecked inequality.

Limiting factors

The idea that unchecked inequality will lead to disaster is not new. In the 19th century, the English political economist David Ricardo and the political philosopher Karl Marx argued that a small elite group would take an ever-increasing share of all that was produced. In Ricardo's case, the elite was the landowners; for Marx, it was the factory owners, the industrial capitalists. Ricardo suggested that, as the population increased, land would become increasingly scarce and therefore more valuable, so landowners would charge higher rents for its use. More and more wealth would flow into the pockets of the landowners.

Marx saw things slightly differently. By the time he was writing, in the mid-19th century, the appalling conditions of the urban poor were everywhere apparent. Land was no longer the focus of attention. Instead, Marx saw the horrific exploitation of children and older factory workers, working long hours in dangerous conditions, living in extreme poverty, while the factory owners were endlessly enriched. He predicted a path of relentless accumulation of capital by the factory owners, which would only end when the desperation of the proletariat (the common people) led them to rebel.

Let it be

The opposite of Ricardo's and Marx's apocalyptic view was that the market would work itself out, given time. This takes the principle of equilibrium and trusts it will be attained if the market is given a chance to find its own level. Adam Smith's 'invisible hand' directing the market would, in this scenario, lead everything to turn out well in the end.

> '*Equality of opportunity as we have known it no longer exists; we are steering a steady course toward economic oligarchy, if we are not there already.*'
>
> Franklin D. Roosevelt, 1932

There are a couple of problems with this theory, not least that it can be inhumane. If it takes 50 years for the market to find its level, millions of people will endure lives of misery and abject poverty while waiting for it to happen. It's also an untested theory – we have to gamble the welfare of the whole world to see if it will eventually turn out to be correct.

Seeing patterns

Economics is based on statistics – data that has been collected and processed rigorously. But such information has only been available for a relatively short time. The USA did not introduce income tax until 1913, so there are no tax returns before this date to show people's level of income. US economists have only

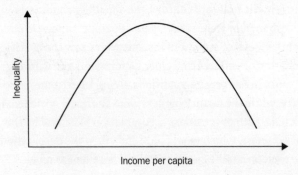

a hundred years' worth of data to work with. In 1955, the American economist Simon Kuznets produced a graph from the data (50 years' worth at that point) which reassuringly showed a bell-shaped curve for inequality. Inequality began at a relatively low level in 1910, then rose to a high point in the 1920s, and fell again in the 1950s. On the basis of this, Kuznets proposed that a growing economy would go through this phase of extreme inequality before settling to a sustainable level of equality.

> '**The development of Modern Industry, therefore, cuts from under its feet the very foundation on which the bourgeoisie produces and appropriates products. What the bourgeoisie produces, above all, are its own gravediggers. Its fall and the victory of the proletariat are equally inevitable.'**
>
> Karl Marx, *Communist Manifesto* (1848)

Whether inequality follows a bell-shape (ending with a low level) or a U-shape (ending with a high level) depends on which bit of curve you look at.

Of course, we still don't know which way it will go next. American economist Thomas Piketty suggests that Kuznets' model was completely wrong, distorted by the impact of two world wars and the intervening economic depression (see the graph below).

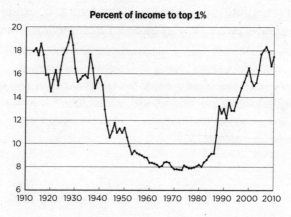

Percent of income to top 1%

The rich get richer . . .

Several economists have suggested that the trend towards the rich accumulating more wealth and the poor becoming poorer is set to continue. Canadian economist Miles Corak has found that as income inequality increases, social mobility falls. Alan B. Krueger, the chairman of the White House Council of Economic Advisers, has called this phenomenon the 'Great Gatsby Curve' – referring to F. Scott Fitzgerald's 1925 novel about self-made millionaire, Jay Gatsby.

In 2008, a cash injection of $700 billion (£453 billion) rescued Wall Street (the New York stock exchange) from the worst consequences of the economic crash. Analysing the outcome, economists Emmanuel Saez and Thomas Piketty found that 93 per cent of the income gains from the 2009–10 recovery went to the top 1 per cent of taxpayers, and 37 per cent went to the top 0.01 per cent – an average of $4.2 million (£2.7m) per wealthy household.

> '*What drags down our entire economy is when there is an ultra-wide chasm between the ultra-wealthy and everyone else.*'
>
> US President Barack Obama, 2012

CRONY CAPITALISM

When close ties between business people and politicians lead to legislation that favours the business agenda, it is often called 'crony capitalism'. It is characterized by policies such as tax breaks for business, selling off national assets to private businesses, government grants to businesses and so on, achieved through lobbying and personal relationships rather than arrived at through a process of independent, objective political and economic reasoning.

CHAPTER 16

Why does the EU pay farmers not to grow crops?

What's the reasoning behind 'set-aside' grants, awarded to farmers for leaving some of their fields empty?

The European Union (EU) has many regulations and policies to help protect traders within member states, but the oddest sounding are the grants paid to farmers *not* to grow crops or keep livestock.

A protective CAP

The Common Agricultural Policy (CAP) was introduced in 1958 to improve efficiency in agriculture in countries of the European Economic Community (EEC). It was intended to guarantee farmers a fair price for their produce, and to benefit consumers by producing higher quantities of better-quality produce. There were five aims:

- to increase the productivity of agriculture
- to ensure a fair standard of living for farmers
- to stabilize the market for agricultural produce
- to guarantee the food supply
- to ensure fair prices for consumers.

The policy guaranteed a minimum price to farmers for their crops, no matter how much they produced. Farmers could choose to sell on the open market (where they might be able to get more than the minimum price) or sell to the EEC. The EEC promised to buy any amount of produce at the guaranteed minimum price, so farmers did not have to worry if trading conditions in the open market were difficult. They could work out their budget based on the price set by the EEC.

In theory, if there was a glut of produce one year, the EEC would buy it and store it until there was a shortage; then it would sell the glut, protecting consumers from higher prices in those times. But the high guaranteed price led to farmers overproducing because they had a guaranteed market for their produce no matter how much they grew.

Butter mountains and milk lakes

Excess production led to 'lakes' of unsold milk and 'mountains' of surplus butter. The EEC was obliged to buy up surplus stocks at the agreed price, but it was left with food that was difficult to dispose of. There were few options – the food could be either:

- thrown away or destroyed
- fed to farm animals
- given or sold cheaply to countries outside the EEC

Destroying food is unpopular, especially when there are people going hungry. Much of the food was sold very cheaply to the USSR and developing economies, and some surplus stock was sold back to EEC farmers to feed to livestock. All these measures caused resentment among EEC consumers, who were paying high prices in the shops for food they had already subsidised through taxes paid to the EEC. The taxes were used firstly to subsidise farmers and secondly to buy up the surplus food.

The system had its drawbacks even in the countries that received the cheap or free food. The farmers could not compete on price, so found it much harder to sell their own produce. Some were driven out of business, adding to those in poverty and creating an uncertain future, given there was no guarantee that the supply of cheap or free food from overseas would not suddenly dry up.

Enough is enough

In 1984, a quota system was introduced to limit the amount of milk produced. Each EEC country was allocated a milk quota, divided between dairy farmers. Farmers could sell their quota on if they did not want to produce that much milk. Quotas provide a cheap way of controlling prices as there is no need to pay subsidies: the limited supply keeps prices high enough.

The EEC also imposed import restrictions in the form of tariffs (taxes). These artificially raise the price of agricultural products from overseas, so are unpopular with farmers elsewhere in the world. The duty on New Zealand lamb, for example, protects European lamb farmers from cheaper competition.

More or less control

Some EU member states, including the UK, are considering leaving the EU and entering into their own, much freer, trade agreement. They argue that the disadvantages of being tied to such a tightly controlling organization outweigh the benefits.

All nations face the same problem of striking a balance between encouraging free trade with other nations to boost their export markets, and discouraging cheap imports, which can put home producers at a disadvantage. The USA, for example, has trade agreements with 20 nations (mainly Canada and those of Latin and South America). It is also negotiating regional trade agreements with the EU (Transatlantic Trade and Investment Partnership) and the Asian and Pacific countries (Trans-Pacific Partnership).

Paid to do nothing

In 1992, the EU introduced set-aside grants. These pay arable farmers to leave land uncultivated to prevent overproduction. If farmers grew all the crops they could, either market prices would be too low to assure them a good level of income, or the EU would have to buy up and dispose of surplus crops. It's easier not to have to deal with the produce in the first place. This is achieved by paying farmers not to grow it, but to leave the land uncultivated (known as 'set-aside'). Farmers have to rotate the unused land to avoid leaving the same areas uncultivated year after year.

Taking the CAP off

Removing the protection of the CAP would force many small farmers out of business because they would not benefit from the economies of scale (see page 156) that large farms enjoy. Some farm relatively poor land – in the Welsh hills, for example – and without subsidies would find it difficult to survive. In a free market these farms would fail, but this would be politically unpopular and perhaps foolhardy in the long-term. A secure food supply within the EU is important. If the EU is unable to provide food for its members in some future war or natural disaster, the region will be forced to buy highly-priced produce on the open market.

Removing subsidies and lifting import restrictions would save a lot of EU money. Some economists suggest that this will not affect the profitability of successful farms, and consumers will be better off because prices will fall. Although removing the subsidy means that farmers who stay in business receive less for their produce, the price of farmland might fall as it would be a less attractive prospect. Small, unproductive farms would leave the market.

ECONOMIES OF SCALE

It is usually more cost-effective to manufacture a large number of items than a small number. The price of production includes the set-up cost (buying and installing machinery, for example), which must be paid no matter how many items are produced, and the price of supplies (such as raw materials), which are usually cheaper when bought in bulk. These 'fixed costs' become cheaper if they can be shared among a larger number of items. This is known as economies of scale.

Countries that benefit most from the CAP, in terms of receiving the largest amount in subsidies, are strongly in favour of keeping the current system and oppose any reduction in subsidies. They include France, where farming makes up a large proportion of the rural economy and where farmers and farm workers consequently represent a powerful lobbying group. Other countries argue that they are being unfairly penalized by having to pay into a scheme from which they get little in return, and which disadvantages their consumers by keeping prices artificially high.

Other CAPs

The USA and Canada also subsidise farmers, though not to the same degree. Subsidies account for around 15 per cent of farmers' income in the USA and 20 per cent in Canada. In the EU, subsidies are around 30 per cent of farm incomes, but elsewhere the proportion is even higher. In Japan, for example, it is over 50 per cent and in Switzerland (which is not part of the EU) it is closer to 70 per cent.

CHAPTER 17

Is cash on the way out?

Has it outlived its usefulness?

As electronic forms of fund transfer take over, 'hard cash' represents an ever-decreasing part of the economy. Despite this, the amount of cash in circulation is growing. Between 2008 and 2013, the value of British sterling bank notes in use increased by 29 per cent, and the value of euros in circulation by 34 per cent. Between 2007 and 2012, the value of US dollars in circulation increased by 42 per cent. With the advent of cashless cards, the increased use of credit and debit cards and a steady increase in purchases online, are the days of cash numbered? And would it matter if they were?

A brief history of cash

Bartering goods is a problematic form of trade (see Chapter 1) as it depends on the two parties wanting comparable items at the same time. For example, a farmer may have piglets which he is anxious to sell before they begin to cost him money to feed, but he may want in return some bags of wheat that have not yet been harvested. Around 8,000 years ago, to resolve this problem, the people of Ancient Sumer, Babylonia and Mesopotamia began to develop a system of clay tablets. The agreed exchange was written on these tablets, called 'bulla'. In this case, the 'price' (two bags of wheat) was marked. Both sides in the transaction kept one half of the tablet and the piglets (in this case) were handed over. Once the wheat was harvested, the pig farmer handed his half of the clay tablet to the wheat farmer and receive his promised two bags of wheat. In time, these clay tablets became tradable in themselves.

In Ancient China, cowrie shells were used as tokens of trade. Around 1000BC, the Chinese switched from using real shells to metal replicas as their pseudo currency. In 800BC they began to adopt 'spade' and 'knife' money – tiny replicas of tools that came in different weights representing different values. Under Emperor Hien Tsung (AD806–21), the Chinese were the first to devise paper banknotes, but they missed out on the first coins, which were most likely produced in Asia Minor around 640BC and made of a silver-gold alloy called electrum. Other parts of the Greek-speaking world soon adopted the idea.

The invention of banknotes came about because there was a shortage of copper needed to mint coins. But the flirtation with paper notes was relatively brief: the ease with which they could be created meant that the authorities gave in to the temptation to print money whenever they needed it, and runaway inflation resulted. As a consequence, the Chinese stopped making banknotes for many centuries.

A PROMISE TO PAY THE BEARER

In Ancient Mesopotamia, clay tablets inscribed in cuneiform with records of the deposit of commodities in state and temple warehouses were used as records of exchange and as a form of 'promissory note'. A record of stored grain could be used to buy something else, and the new recipient could use the tablet to reclaim the deposited goods. The earliest surviving legal code, the Babylonian code of Hammurabi from 1760BC, regulates the use and trade of these contracts.

The first European banknotes were issued in Sweden in 1661 by Stockholm banker Johan Palmstruch, with the approval of the Swedish government. He, too, soon printed more money than he could redeem from his deposits of silver. He was prosecuted for fraud in 1668 and sentenced to death (though the sentence was later commuted to imprisonment).

HACKSILVER

Hacksilver, as the name suggests, is a form of currency made by hacking silver into pieces. Norsemen commonly used it as currency, along with coins, as it came from the spoils of their raids. Silver objects – plates, jewellery, devotional items – were broken into pieces, valued by weight and used in trade and commerce. The name of the Russian currency unit, the rouble, is derived from the verb рубить (*rubit*), meaning 'to chop'.

The gold standard

The banknote's poor track record couldn't stop the march of progress. It became impossible for precious metals alone to fulfil the demands for cash, so the first national banks sprang up and began issuing promissory notes more reliable than those of Palmstruch. Even so, the danger of inflation, largely kept in check by the 'gold standard', remained. The gold standard tied each nation's currency to the price of gold, which was set independently. Effectively it meant there was a fixed exchange rate. In the USA, from 1834 to 1933, the price of gold was at $20.67 per ounce, while in the UK it was £3 17s 10½d. This meant £1 was worth $4.867. It worked as long as no participating country decided massively to overprint money.

The gold standard broke down around World War I, when nations printed extra money to finance their war efforts. It was reinstated after the war. Britain left the gold standard in 1931 during an economic downturn, when a run on sterling made it impossible to maintain the price of the pound without depleting the country's gold reserves. This allowed the pound to be devalued and the British economy to recover. The gold standard eventually collapsed in 1971 when the USA withdrew its promise to redeem overseas dollar holdings in gold at $35 (£22.50) an ounce (part of the Bretton Woods system of 1944, see Chapter 22).

> **POUND FOR POUND**
>
> The British 'pound sterling' is the oldest established currency in use. The pound has existed since 1560, when Queen Elizabeth I set its value at one troy pound (about 373 grams) of silver. The term 'sterling' first appeared in 1078 and denoted the purest form of silver available (around 99 per cent pure, also known as 'fine silver').

Going . . .

We could argue that the heyday of cash ended with the emergence of cheques. The Romans used something similar, called *praescriptiones*, in the 1st century BC, and 9th century Arabs and medieval Europeans used similar bills of exchange.

The earliest surviving modern-style cheque is handwritten and dates from 1659. The Bank of England was the first to issue pre-printed forms for writing cheques, introducing them in 1717. The real boom in cheque use, however, came after 1959, when a machine-readable character set made it possible to process large numbers of cheques automatically. With the advent of cheque guarantee cards in 1969, retailers were assured that cheques would be honoured, even if the account holder did not have the funds. (The bank took responsibility to reclaim the money from the account holder.) The surge in the use of cheques peaked in the 1980s and 1990s in most countries, when they became the next most popular method of payment after good old cash. Although billions of cheques were processed each year, cash still held its own.

. . . going . . .

Banks phased out cheque guarantee cards during the mid-1990s, replacing them with debit cards. Customers still had to sign their name for each transaction, just as with a cheque. Debit and credit cards were fitted with an electronic microchip on which was stored a personal identification number (or PIN). This system was called 'chip and PIN'. The method was considered more secure as it needed no signature (which could be forged) and the PIN was known only to the cardholder.

The trend towards online purchases, electronic bank transfers and secure online payment options such as Paypal also knocked a huge dent in the use of cash. Now, instead of paying in a shop with cash, people were increasingly paying online by card or Paypal for goods that could come from anywhere in the world, with no need to convert between currencies. Debit and credit cards can also be used internationally, so travellers have less need to carry foreign currencies.

. . . gone?

Purchasing by contactless payment cards and mobile phone or other handheld devices means there is still less need to carry cash today – even to buy small-value items. A few statistics show how the use of cash has declined:

- The value of payments made using cash has been well below the value of cashless payments for a long time. Credit and debit card sales overtook cash sales in the UK in 2003.
- In 2015, the value of debit and credit card consumer sales was three times that of cash sales.

- Early in March 2015, the number of UK transactions carried out using cash fell below the number using cashless payment methods for the first time.
- If we include all transactions, including those between large organizations and banks, the value of cash transactions in the UK in 2014 was £260 billion ($400bn). But the value of automated transactions was £76,643 billion ($118bn) – nearly 30 times as much.

Filthy lucre

Cash is heavy and insecure (it can be lost or stolen). It takes more effort to count out and check cash than to wave a card, and it's dirty – a card that has only been in your own possession seems more hygienic.

Most people have heard the urban legend that banknotes are contaminated with cocaine. A study in 1994 by the 9th Circuit Court of Appeals in Los Angeles, USA, found that three out of four banknotes were contaminated with cocaine or other illicit drugs. There have been similar findings elsewhere; a UK-wide study found a contamination rate of 80 per cent. In London in 1999 it was even worse – only four out of 500 banknotes tested were cocaine-free. During the SARS epidemic of 2003, China took the precaution of quarantining banknotes – those that were paid into banks were held for 24 hours before being released again (the SARS virus does not survive long outside a living cell).

The last to go

People still use cash for shopping, but in ever decreasing numbers. Parking meters, vending machines and other mechanical payment devices are increasingly being converted to accept payment by phone or card. Buses and other forms of public transport still accept cash in many places (though

London's buses have been cash-free since 2014), but contactless payment cards are becoming more common. The days of the cash-based vending machine are probably numbered too, as coins and notes are expensive to collect and bank. Currently, independent traders such as corner shop owners, newsagents and market and street vendors still prefer to deal in cash because of the high cost of the levy imposed by credit card companies and banks. And there is the underworld: traders who demand cash payments to avoid tax liability, for example.

FALLING APART

Germany had a problem with the literal disintegration of its currency when some euro notes started to crumble after being withdrawn from ATMs. It transpired that the notes had been contaminated with Eastern European crystal meth, which contains a high level of sulphates. This mixed with the sweat from people handling the cash to produce sulphuric acid, which broke down the fabric of the notes.

One of the great advantages of cash is that it's anonymous. But its diminished use now makes paying for an expensive object with cash look a little suspicious. In a bizarre twist of history, it seems that carrying cash – once the mark of wealth – is now a sign of being on the margins of society, and possibly even quite poor.

In Sweden (which has gone furthest towards a cash-free economy), the number of bank robberies fell dramatically as electronic payment methods took over – from 110 in 2008 to just 16 three years later. Most Swedish banks simply don't handle cash any more. This trend is being adopted in UK and European banks, as indicated by the removal of security screens that are now considered unnecessary because cashiers no longer handle large amounts of cash.

Is it worth it?

Cash costs a lot to manufacture and distribute: shops have to pay for secure storage and secure movement to the bank where it is deposited; handling and moving cash takes time; and counterfeit money is a burden on those who innocently accept it. A 2015 study found that if the USA abandoned cash, GDP would increase by 0.47 per cent. It doesn't sound much, but as GDP for the year was said to be $17.710 trillion (£11.5 trillion), 0.47 per cent of that amount represents $83.237 billion (£54bn).

The cost of cash is highest for consumers in countries with negative interest rates, such as Denmark and Switzerland (as of 2018). This means that depositors have to pay just to keep their money in the bank. In Denmark, an interest rate for depositors of -0.65 per cent means it really is more prudent for people to keep their cash under the mattress.

TOP CASH-POOR COUNTRIES

Among the countries where cash is becoming obsolete, Sweden leads the way with only 3 per cent of transactions carried out in cash. Somaliland (an autonomous region of Somalia) is not far behind. Purchases with mobile phones are more common there than almost anywhere else in the world, with even street vendors taking payment by phone.

In Kenya, the M-pesa mobile money system has 15 million users. It's used not just for small payments, but for salaries, school fees and routine bills.

Canada decided to stop printing currency from 2012, using plastic bills instead (though they are still cash). Most Canadians (56 per cent) would sooner use an electronic wallet than cash.

Experts predict that the first totally cashless country will appear by 2030, if not before.

CHAPTER 18

How do economic crashes happen?

The fragility of the world's money markets became painfully apparent in 2008.

In 2008, the flourishing economic growth seen over the previous decade was at an almost steroid-fuelled pace. The failure of IndyMac Bank in the USA was the first sign that things were going horribly wrong in the financial markets. More banks and financial institutions followed IndyMac into collapse and the effect of this spread quickly around the world. The impact on businesses and individuals soon became catastrophic. Although governments bailed out some major financial institutions to prevent a complete collapse of the banking system, the crash led to a worldwide recession worse than any since the Great Depression of the 1930s.

Money for nothing

Economists argue over the exact mix of the complex and interrelated causes of this crash, but there is general agreement that greed, over-confidence and too little regulation in the financial sector allowed a vast and precarious market to build on very insecure foundations. The value of the financial markets was, in fact, many times greater than the value of the real goods and services underlying it.

The recession began with housing, and a decline in real estate values in the USA in 2007. But before that, the scene for disaster had been set by banks creating too much extra money through making loans incautiously. Each time a bank lends money, it essentially creates money from nowhere (see Chapter 9).

In the years 2000–2007, the amount of money and debt in the UK economy doubled, but only 8 per cent of the 'new' money went into industries outside the financial sector. The remainder went into the following: residential property (around 31 per cent), commercial property (20 per cent); the financial markets (32 per cent); personal loans and credit cards (8 per cent). Other economies followed a similar pattern.

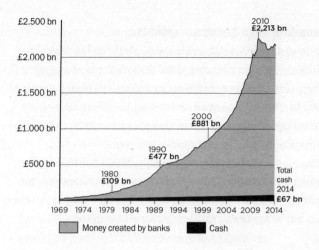

£2.500 bn

£2.000 bn

£1.500 bn

£1.000 bn

£500 bn

2010
£2,213 bn

2000
£881 bn

1990
£477 bn

1980
£109 bn

Total
cash
2014

£67 bn

1969 1974 1979 1984 1989 1994 1999 2004 2009 2014

Money created by banks   Cash

Subprime mortgages

In the past, if a potential house buyer wanted to take out a
mortgage, the lender would assess the value of the property,
the income of the applicant and their ability to pay the
mortgage instalments. If the applicant's salary was too low,
meaning they might struggle to keep up the repayments, or if
they had a bad credit record, so might default, or if the house
seemed overpriced and might decline in value over time, the
loan was refused. This made financial sense.

During the 1990s, as housing was in demand, the price for
real estate climbed steadily. Financiers did not see why the
trend would not continue. This made lending to buy housing,
even risky lending, look attractive. Some American banks
began to offer high-risk loans – lending money to people with
a higher-than-average chance of defaulting. These became
known as 'subprime' mortgages. It was assumed that houses
would always increase in price so, if the client defaulted, the
house could be repossessed and sold to cover the outstanding
loan. It seemed like a fool-proof method of generating extra
income for the banks at little additional risk.

Spreading eggs between baskets

The banks believed that risky debts would be less risky if bundled together, so they pooled the subprime mortgages. The theory was that even if real-estate values fell in one region of the USA, they would not in others. By bundling loans from around the nation, risk would be spread and local fluctuations in the market would make little difference.

The pooled mortgages were used to back securities called Collateralized Debt Obligations (CDOs). They were divided into tranches based on assessed risk. This meant that all the least-likely-to-default mortgages were bundled together, all the most-likely-to-default were bundled together, and there were plenty of other bundles in between. Those considered most secure were given a triple-A rating, indicating that they were a safe bet. The rating was given by trusted agents who were in the pay of the banks which had created the CDOs. Unsurprisingly, they were overgenerous in their assessment of security.

The market for those baskets

As interest rates were low, investors were keen to find options paying a higher-than-average rate. The CDOs were that option. The risk was well-hidden within the pooling and tranching, and the final product seemed far removed from the struggling individuals who in earlier years would never have been given a mortgage in the first place. But the whole edifice was built on these people in their insecure homes.

The CDOs were such an attractive proposition that many investors leveraged money to buy them – borrowing at a low interest rate to invest at a higher one, with the expectation of profiting from the difference. However, if the investment wasn't paid off, the loan still had to be repaid. The CDOs were traded between institutions in the USA and internationally.

The baskets break

When American property prices fell, the system of CDOs collapsed. And the decline in property values didn't just happen sporadically in different regions, it happened everywhere. As borrowers defaulted, the fragile subprime mortgages fell victim to the downturn. Neither the home-owners nor the banks could sell the houses for a high enough price to cover the value of the loan. As house prices tumbled, there was a massive problem with negative equity – the value of the homes was now lower than the mortgages taken out to buy them.

LEVERAGING (ALSO 'GEARING')

Leverage is a technique used to maximize profits or losses. Typically, it involves gambling with interest rates or the values and future values of products or commodities. A person putting down a deposit on a house and taking out a mortgage is leveraging their savings – they gamble on the assumption that the value of the house will rise over time, so they will end up with more, rather than less, equity.

Negative equity only becomes an issue when the owner needs to sell because he or she will not be able to repay their debt. High-risk borrowers defaulted on their mortgages because they could not simply sell and move. The mortgage lenders stood to lose money and this meant the CDOs lost value. No matter that the CDOs had been pooled and tranched – they were not as safe as the banks had claimed they would be, and soon they were worthless. If they changed hands at all, they sold for rock-bottom prices.

The banks saw their capital value fall. This happened even though most of the borrowers at the bottom of the chain (the mortgage holders) might not even have defaulted. The market was based on the assumption that they wouldn't, and the value of that assumption had plummeted. It was, in effect, a market built on nothing.

Liquidity crisis

The collapse of subprime mortgages led to a liquidity crisis. Financial institutions struggled to convert the assets they held in the form of loans (and, increasingly, repossessed houses) into cash. After their fall in value, the houses on which people had defaulted were often worth less than the money loaned to buy them. Even if the banks managed to sell the houses, in an increasingly depressed market, they would still not recover all the money they were owed.

Credit default swaps were another weak link in the chain. These insurance policies were taken out to guard against borrowers defaulting on repayments. So, if you loaned a friend $1,000, you might take out insurance to cover non-repayment of the loan. If your friend defaulted, the insurance would pay out. If your friend didn't default, the insurer would keep the money you had paid. With credit default swaps, as soon as the chain started to break, insurers and banks crumbled under the burden of pay-outs. Just days after Lehman Brothers declared bankruptcy (see box on page 174), the insurance company AIG also collapsed, brought down by the mass of credit-default risk it had insured.

The collapse of Lehman Brothers was a disaster not only for its employees and investors, but also for the wider economy. With the realization that even the biggest banks might be allowed to go under, all financial institutions panicked and stopped lending money. Without access to loans, even those businesses who had managed their finances responsibly found themselves in difficulty. They might simply have wanted to borrow money as part of a managed plan for expansion, or in the short term as part of an established operating pattern, but the banks were no longer willing to lend, even to safe creditors. The situation snowballed, businesses slowed down or were unable to borrow to fund day-to-day transactions, and they began laying off workers. As unemployment grew, people were buying less, manufacturing declined even further and more people were laid off. In this way the recession unfolded.

Although banks lacked the confidence or funds to lend to borrowers, they still expected the businesses and individuals they had financed to repay the loans and interest owing. Just as a bank making a loan creates money, repaying a loan destroys money. With the repayment of loans, money was being taken out of the economy.

Bailing out and clawing back

To prevent a catastrophic collapse of the economy, the major Western governments were forced to bail out the large banks. Governments deemed these banks to be 'too big to fail' so had to provide the money they needed, sometimes by nationalizing them (taking them into public ownership). To fund these measures, the governments themselves had to borrow money, for example, by issuing bonds. This led to huge national debts. To repay these debts, the governments made cuts in public funding, resulting in a reduction in public services and welfare/benefit payments, which became known as 'austerity measures'.

Who's to blame?

Clearly the banks and the finance industry were at fault. They had taken on large amounts of debt to finance investment without being sure they

> '*If you owe the bank $100, that's your problem. If you owe the bank $100 million, that's the bank's problem.*'
>
> J. Paul Getty, rephrasing an old saying

THE DEMISE OF LEHMAN BROTHERS

The US bank Lehman Brothers was the first major institution to become a casualty of the financial crisis. By 2007, Lehman Brothers was leveraged to a ratio of 31:1 (assets: owners' equity) meaning that it actually owned less than a thirtieth of its apparent assets and the remainder was based on borrowing. In particular, Lehman Brothers was overexposed in the subprime mortgage market. It had leveraged its capital to such an extent that even a slight downturn in the value of its assets (just 3–4 per cent) was enough to wipe out its entire value and led to its collapse in 2008.

had enough wiggle-room to absorb any losses or shifts in the market. Greed, complacency and misplaced trust were at the root of the problem.

Banks don't operate in a vacuum, however. Regulators and central banks should be supervising them and preventing excesses which can lead to disaster. As early as 2005, a savings glut (financed largely by Asia and Europe) had been producing very low interest rates. This fed the desire to seek out higher risk, higher yield investments. But regulators did not heed the warnings. Most catastrophically, regulators in the USA did not step in to save Lehman Brothers.

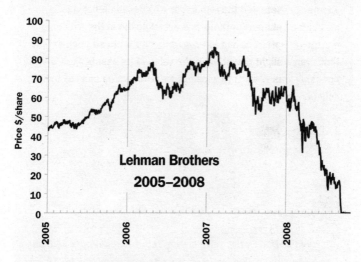

Economists are divided about how far they hold different parties responsible. Right-wing economists tend to blame the US government and the housing policy that encouraged subprime lending. Left-wing economists tend to blame the greed of the financial institutions and under-regulation of the financial markets. Discovering the true reason or reasons for the crash might help to avoid another crash in the future.

'Your company is now bankrupt, our economy is in crisis, but you get to keep $480 million (£276 million). I have a very basic question for you: is this fair?'

US Congressman Henry Waxman to Richard Fuld, CEO of Lehman Brothers, at the Committee on Oversight and Government Reform

THE HIGH PRICE OF BAIL-OUT

The sum used to bail out British banks in 2009 was the most ever spent by the UK government in such a way. Until then, the largest sum paid out was in 1834, when Britain's 46,000 slave owners received compensation following the abolition of slavery.

The sum paid to British slave owners represented 40 per cent of government spending for 1834 and was equivalent to £16–17 billion ($24–26bn) today.

CHAPTER 19

Does austerity work?

Stimulus or austerity? Which is the best remedy for an economy in recession?

Starting with the problem

An economy in recession is sluggish, with little activity, often high in debt and low in spending. It is not economically productive – it has very low growth, no growth or negative growth (meaning the economy is shrinking). A widespread (though simplistic) definition of recession is two consecutive quarters (of a year) of falling GDP. Some economists cite a rise in unemployment of 1.5–2 per cent over a year as another sign of recession.

Recession can become a vicious circle and a downward spiral. When people don't spend money, businesses make less of it. With less income from sales, businesses can't afford staff, so unemployment grows. People in jobs are nervous and those without jobs can't afford to buy as much, so spending falls again. This is called the negative multiplier effect. The further drop in demand prompts businesses to cut back more, and as a result some businesses fail. Further job losses mean that spending falls again. In a country with a welfare state which supports no- or low-income people, recession increases the need for benefits, so raises government spending.

Falling profits, rising unemployment, or a reduction in spending and wages mean that less is collected in taxes. The government has to pay out more in benefits, but is collecting less income, which leads to a deficit. The government might cut spending in other areas, such as road-building or defence, but this pushes those sectors into recession, too. If the government borrows money, it then has to pay it back, and pay interest on the loans. It can be hard to see a way out.

Spend, spend, spend

One way of tackling recession is for a government to stimulate the economy by injecting cash into it. For example, a government can increase public spending by building more roads and railway lines and by expanding education and healthcare. This employs labour and creates a demand for goods and raw materials. Although the money has to be borrowed or created to do this, it is going directly into the economy. Employment rises, people have the confidence to spend, and the economy becomes more productive because of improved conditions. At first, people might remain anxious and they may save the extra money rather than spend it. But eventually spending grows and more money goes into circulation, which leads to increased output from industry and a rise in jobs. Banks have the confidence to loan money to industry to fund expansion, and money comes into the economy to help fund the government's debt.

In time, the theory goes, people are earning and spending, so they are paying more in taxes and the government starts to recoup the money it has spent. As the economy picks up, the artificial stimulus is needed less and government spending can return to normal levels.

Belt-tightening time

An alternative to stimulus is austerity, when the government reduces spending and, as a consequence, many people in the country also reduce their spending. To save money, a government can cut spending on welfare and on public goods and services. It can also limit public sector pay and pensions and reduce the interest paid on government securities. These measures immediately reduce the amount the government has to pay out, but mean that many people have less to spend. The drop in spending can make the situation worse in the short term, as the economy slows down further and government income from taxes drops. The savings made by cutting public spending can then be used to reduce taxation on businesses and individuals in the private sector. The theory is that this will lead to an increase in general spending, as people pay less in taxes and have more to spend. Businesses grow, employment increases and foreign trade expands. Money raised from cuts in one area of public spending can also be used to pay for growth in another, such as road and rail building and other areas of infrastructure. This boosts employment and increases spending and taxation. Obviously government can only use the money it has saved in these ways, as a stimulus, if it does not already have large debts to finance and pay back. An economy in crisis, such as the Greek economy in the second decade of the 21st century, might resort to imposing strict austerity measures just to pay back debts, with no intention of funding public spending or tax cuts.

Austerity and war

Many economies imposed austerity programmes during the two world wars of the 20th century. In these cases, the government needed to raise (or save) money to fund an expensive war effort and secure essential food and other services while a portion of the population was away fighting. In 1919, in the aftermath of World War I, the USA imposed a top income tax rate of 77 per cent. The government took control of the food supply and fixed the prices of staple foods and other essential items. Fuel use was banned on certain days, and daylight saving time introduced. But an economy following a war is very different from an economy in recession. The US economy had been booming before the war, and popular support for the war effort made for a more positive spirit among the population than the ground-down weariness of people who have faced long-term hardship. When war came again in 1939, it actually helped to lift some economies out of recession or depression, as it brought demand for goods and services, and increased employment.

Lessons from history

Before the crash of 2008, the last major world recession was the Great Depression of the 1930s. It came about after the American stock market on Wall Street crashed spectacularly in 1929. To protect American producers, the USA called in overseas loans and imposed barriers to imports. The result was that the depression spread to other parts of the world, particularly Europe.

By 1933, 13–15 million Americans (20 per cent of the population) were unemployed and nearly half the nation's banks had failed. The situation was disastrous. Many people lost their savings, jobs and homes when the banks crashed, and some took their own lives in despair. Farming had been in crisis in the USA for years, caused in part by the switch to inappropriate farming methods which had led to severe drought. The USA had less welfare support than the UK and the situation for many people was desperate.

During the Depression, tenant farmers could not repay loans to banks, their farms were repossessed and workers were laid off. This led to further unemployment and the mass movement of people between states.

One approach

In Britain, the 'heavy' industries of ship-building, coal-mining and steel-smelting, mainly concentrated in Wales, northern England and Scotland, were the first to fail. In the town of Jarrow, every single adult male was unemployed. In the south of England, however, the newer 'light' industries were much less badly affected, leading to severe north–south inequality. The government increased taxes and cut unemployment benefits to try to reduce its spending. It also imposed import duties, which were intended to protect British industry, but led to a further downturn in trade as other countries retaliated with their own import tariffs. These austerity measures possibly made matters worse.

At the same time, some government actions helped the situation. They increased the amount of money in circulation and reduced interest rates, encouraging people who had the money to spend it. (There is little incentive to save if interest rates are low.) Government used incentives to encourage industries to start up or move to depressed areas and provide employment. And incentives were used to build 500,000 new homes, which not only provided much-needed housing but also created jobs and demand for materials, invigorating the economy. This is an example of cuts in one area of public spending being used to fund increased spending in another.

Another approach

After a few years, the USA switched to stimulus. The president at the start of the Depression was J. Edgar Hoover. He believed the recession would run its course and the economy would naturally recover. He tried to bail out some of the banks with government loans in the hope that the effect would 'trickle down' to working people. As a Republican, he firmly believed in a free-market economy and that government should not intervene in its workings.

In 1932, Hoover lost the presidential election to Democrat Franklin D. Roosevelt. By the time Roosevelt was inaugurated in 1933, all the banks had closed and the government did not have the money to pay its own employees.

In the slump of the 1930s, starving people queued for food at soup kitchens.

Roosevelt introduced emergency measures to stabilize the banks still considered sound and launched his 'New Deal'. This provided jobs and stimulus through massive government projects, such as the building of dams and hydroelectric power stations, which would make other industries possible in depressed areas. Although recovery was not smooth, it was substantial. The end of World War II finally marked the end of the Depression.

What will work now?

Austerity and stimulus have been used in varying degrees by different nations to confront the economic crisis that began in 2008. Economists disagree about what, if anything, is working.

President Franklin D. Roosevelt

The verdict of the International Monetary Fund (IMF) is that austerity doesn't work. Those countries that have adopted predominantly austere measures have fared worse than those that have opted for stimulus – spending their way out of recession. In 2013, the chief economist of the IMF, Olivier Blanchard, accused the UK government of 'playing with fire' by continuing to pursue austerity measures. In 2015, however, the managing director of the IMF, Christine Lagarde, said the UK authorities had managed to provide the right balance of spending cuts and revenue raising: '. . . when we look at the comparative growth rates delivered by various countries in Europe, it's obvious that what's happening in the UK has actually worked.'

Only time will tell who was right.

> **'The only thing we have to fear is fear itself.'**
>
> Franklin D. Roosevelt,
> US presiden

CHAPTER 20

How long will the shops stay open?

In the past 20 years, some major stores have closed their doors for the last time. Does it matter that they have gone?

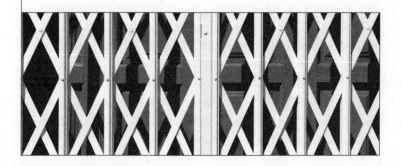

One in nine working Americans is employed in retail. Between 1950 and 1990, jobs in this sector grew at a rate 50 per cent above general employment, but since 1990 retail jobs have grown half as fast as jobs in other sectors. A similar pattern is seen elsewhere in the world. What has happened to this, until recently, the steadiest of industries?

Late, great industries

Other industries have suffered similar declines in the past (see Chapter 10). First agriculture and then the manufacturing industries were subject to falling labour as mechanization and efficiency increased. At the start of the 20th century, more than 40 per cent of Americans worked in agriculture. Today, the USA produces more food than it did a hundred years ago, although less than 2 per cent of the population works in farming. Manufacturing employs about 10 per cent of Americans compared with around 30 per cent ten years ago; and it looks as though retail might be the next sector of the economy to face declining employment.

Window shopping and Windows shopping

One of the biggest changes has been the internet revolution, with the result that a lot of retailing is now carried out online. Online shopping gives us more choice, often lower prices, and saves us having to venture out to buy what we want. One disadvantage is the need to wait in for delivery, but even that problem is fast disappearing as more businesses offer a network of local collection points. By 2015, around 12 per cent of purchases in the UK were online, a quarter of these through Amazon, the United States' largest online retailer. Amazon's rise has been meteoric, from 19 billion US sales in 2008 to over 61 billion sales four years later. Its founder, Jeff Bezos, has an estimated net worth of $156 billion (£121 billion).

The profitable few

Amazon staff who are employed to pack and dispatch orders earn an average annual salary of $21,687 (£16,800). But the average income that each full-time employee generated *for* Amazon was $600,000 (£390,000)in 2014 , down from over $1 million (£650,000) in 2011. This is three times the average sum a traditional retailer gains from a full-time employee.

Until recently, customers preferred to buy goods such as furniture, clothes and shoes in store, where they could examine them first hand. But there has been a growing trend for shoppers to browse in real shops and then order their chosen item more cheaply online. The growth in shopping comparison websites and smartphones has meant that people can even do this from their phones while standing in the shop. To counter this trend, many shops now have their own websites, which offer goods more cheaply than in-store; some also offer a click-and-collect service.

WHERE DO YOU WORK?

Top employment sectors in the USA (2013):
1 Retail trade
2 Accommodation and food services
3 Professional and technical services
4 Administrative and waste services
5 Education (local public elementary/primary and secondary schools)

Reassuringly for the traditional retail trade, shoppers are more likely to make impulse buys in a shop than online.

The Walmart effect

Online shopping is not the only blow to conventional retailing. The so-called 'Walmart effect' captures the impact of massive low-end retailers moving into a local market. Walmart is a chain of discount department stores and retail warehouses based in the USA. When Walmart opens a store, it can save low-income families living in the area up to 30 per cent on their food bills. Its low prices also help to bring down the prices of other stores in the area, which are forced to compete. There are, inevitably, other consequences: a study in 2008 found that for every job created in a new Walmart store, 1.4 retail jobs are lost as other stores close or downsize.

Self-service and no service

In the 20th century, shopping had already undergone a major revolution with the introduction of self-service, initially in grocery stores. During the first half of that century, most shoppers were served personally by a shop assistant. The idea of touching goods unsupervised was unthinkable. Other customers waited patiently in line until a staff member became free. But this was not economic as it limited the number of sales, especially in busy periods. Employing extra staff to cope with the rush meant they were not working, and not making money for the store, at other times.

This began to change with the introduction of 'self-service', pioneered by US entrepreneur Clarence Saunders who opened his first 'Piggly Wiggly' self-service grocery store in 1916. The concept soon spread throughout the USA and beyond. Self-service increased sales dramatically as retail staff were needed only to take payment at the checkout and to stock shelves. By 1951, the UK's Premier chain of self-service supermarkets was taking ten times as much as equivalent traditional British grocery stores.

Now nearly all shops are fully or partly self-service. The introduction of self-service checkouts and hand-held scanning devices has cut staff and therefore costs even further. The boundary between online and real-world shopping is blurring: online orders are delivered to a nearby store for collection; out-of-stock items can be ordered online in store; and customers can compare prices over the phone while standing in a shop.

Two markets

Increasingly, high street shopping has become polarized. At the budget end of the market, everything is low price; at the 'high end', quality, exclusivity and customer service have the most impact on purchasing decisions. The minimalist styling of the Apple Store is an example of this trend where customer service and image are all-important. The space is not used efficiently; only a handful of products are on show, albeit in different colours and configurations. Accessories are placed discreetly against the walls, leaving most of the floor space free so that people can worship the elegant, stylish technology. The staff are attentive and knowledgeable.

At the other end of the scale, discount stores prioritize low price and abundance of choice. This approach was pioneered in the UK by East End trader Jack Cohen, founder of the Tesco supermarket chain, whose slogan 'pile it high, sell it cheap' has been adopted by clothes shops such as Primark and general stores such as Poundland. Queues are often long (because the shops are popular), and the shop floor is noisy and crowded.

How can stores like Primark afford to sell things so cheaply? They manufacture in areas of the world where labour is cheap, but so do a lot of the more expensive brands. They only sell their own branded goods, so there is no intermediary taking a share. They place bulk orders, so benefit from economies of scale (see Chapter 16); their production processes are highly efficient; they use cheap raw materials; they don't run expensive advertising campaigns; their stores make economic use of floor space. This is in total contrast to Apple Store.

The squeezed middle

Today, some of the middle-grade shops are threatened – those serving the now-struggling middle classes. High-end retailers catering to the wealthy have been largely unaffected by recent economic conditions because the income of the wealthiest consumers has not dropped. Discount and budget retailers have seen business increase because middle-class shoppers have moved down-market as their incomes have dropped.

Does it matter?

Who loses out if shops close? Most obviously, the people who own them and those who work there. Retail jobs are relatively low-paid and low-skilled. This type of job is considered by economists to be fungible (see Chapter 12). The difficulty arises when there are not enough jobs to swap into.

There is an impact on cityscapes, too. Closing shops and empty units mean fewer people are attracted into town centres and shopping malls. Reduced footfall leads to further shops closing, and so on.

The rise of the online retailer

While online shopping may have hit the traditional retail sector hard, it has opened up new opportunities for those willing to take advantage of them. Many people now sell goods and services from home, through their own websites or giant online outlets such as Amazon and eBay. The start-up costs and annual overheads involved in working from home are minimal compared to those associated with opening and running a traditional shop. There is less need to take out expensive loans (with the high risk of bankruptcy if the business fails) and this gives many more people the confidence to start their own business. Online shopping has also provided work for (therefore jobs in) courier and delivery services.

CHAPTER 21

How does the stock market work?

The stock market is at the heart of national economics. But what does it actually do?

15,000	0.10 ▲	+ 1.82
100,000	361.80 ▼	− 0.60
30,000	0.25 ▼	− 1.39
800,000	6.22 ▼	− 1.80
4,100,000	247.30 ▼	− 0.53
26,000	20.18 ▼	− 0.57
12,000	100.41 ▼	− 0.36
3,000,000	203.99 ▼	− 0.29

The stock market allows people and organizations to trade in little portions of companies. These portions – called stocks and shares – entitle the owner to have a say in how a company is run and/or claim a dividend. Dividends are a payout representing a portion of the company's profits.

Sharing a company

Imagine you wanted to start a business making giant kites. Setting it up would incur certain costs, including:

- renting premises in which to conduct business
- sourcing materials and processes
- hiring and paying the workers
- marketing the kites
- distributing or delivering the kites
- running the business (administration, accounting, and so on)
- paying taxes and costs associated with the workers (pension contributions, health insurance, sick pay, and so on).

You could start on a small scale and take on more staff as the orders grew, or you could start at a more ambitious level and seek investment capital. If you chose the second path, you might borrow money from friends and family or from the bank, or you might look for outside investors to give you money in exchange for a share in the company. Some businesses can only be started on a large scale, with investment capital. If, instead of making kites, you wanted to make planes or start a telecoms network, you would probably not fund it from your own pocket or from a bank loan.

An investor won't lend money unless they believe the business will make a profit and give them a return on their investment. The investor might also expect to have a say in the running of the company, because they won't want to risk losing their money through poor business decisions. To secure their claim on any profit and have some input into how you run the business, they buy a share of it.

Stocks and shares

The total capital (assets) of a company, which can be divided between the owners if the company goes into liquidation, is called its stock, or capital stock. A portion of a company sold to an investor is called a share. There are many different types of shares. Common or ordinary shares entitle the owner to have a say in how the company is run, to be paid a dividend each year, and to own a share of the assets. If a company starts with a stock-holding of 1,000 shares, someone who buys 100 shares will own 10 per cent of the company. He or she will also have 10 per cent of the votes at shareholder meetings where company policy and plans are discussed, will gain 10 per cent of the shared-out profits, and will have a claim to 10 per cent of the company's assets.

Another type of share, called a preferred share, offers no voting rights but pays a higher dividend and has a preferential claim on assets. If the company were to fail and go into liquidation, the preferred shareholders would receive their share of the stock before ordinary shareholders. Together, the shareholders own the company.

More investment

Start-up is not the only point at which a company might need investment capital. If your kite-making business went well, you might want to move to larger premises or order new machinery. You could raise money (capital stock) by selling shares. The new shareholders would also have rights over the assets, rights to dividends, and perhaps votes in board meetings. Before new shares can be issued, the existing shareholders have to agree to the move because it reduces the value of their own shares. They are often given first refusal: the right to buy the new shares before they are offered to anyone else. It might seem unwise to issue more shares, but it is done to increase the company's profitability so that everyone will benefit in the long run (at least, that's the idea).

Private and public companies

Your kite-making business might start off as a private limited company. This means its shares are not traded on the open market, but you can offer them to people of your choice. Sale of shares can be restricted, so none of the shareholders is allowed unilaterally to sell their shares to just anyone. Although this limits the pool of available investors, it means it's easier to keep control of the company.

Large corporations are often public limited companies (or public traded companies in the USA). Their shares are traded on the open market and listed on the appropriate stock market. Anyone can buy shares. This means that unless the original owners keep at least 51 per cent of the shareholding themselves, they can lose control of the company because others can unite to vote against them in shareholder meetings. Shareholders direct the course a company takes. Sometimes the founders of a company are dismissed by shareholders acting in unison against them.

Buying and selling

When shares are listed on the stock market, they can be traded openly, meaning they are bought and sold by stockbrokers and investors. The selling price of shares is an indication of the financial health of the company. Suppose shares in your kite-making business originally sold for $10 each. The company gets off to a good start and at the end of the year the value of its capital (stock) has increased by 20 per cent. This means the value of each share has also increased by 20 per cent. Someone who wanted to sell their shares should be able to get $12 for each of them. That's a good return on a single year's investment.

Shares are a risky investment, however. If the business does badly and loses value, the shares will be worth less than the shareholder paid for them. For this reason, shares should be regarded as a long-term investment.

Provided the business is basically sound, short-term fluctuations in the price of shares can be ignored as, over time, the shares should increase in value. This is the traditional attitude towards buying and trading in shares, but the current stock market has many different types of investor, some of whom have very short-term aims.

STEVE JOBS

Steve Jobs and Steve Wozniak founded Apple Computers in 1976, but needed to raise funds to promote their first serious computer, the Apple II. To do so, they sold shares the following year. They sold so many that they lost control of the company six years later. Investors felt that Jobs was too young and inexperienced to run a large company and in 1983 John Sculley, previously boss of Pepsi, was appointed to head it up. Sculley and Jobs clashed frequently, and in 1985 Jobs left and started a new computer company called NeXT. A series of executives then ran Apple, but were not sufficiently innovative or imaginative to reinvigorate the company. Eventually, Apple bought up NeXT – and Jobs. From 2000, Jobs ran Apple again, seeing it go from strength to strength and adding new markets to its portfolio.

Round and round

Share value is also affected by the price for which the shares change hands. This looks like a circular argument, and it is. If the company is seen to be doing well, there will be demand for its shares, so their price goes up. If the company is seen to be doing badly, the share price falls and nervous investors sell. There is an oversupply of shares and little demand for them, so the price drops further.

At this point, when the share price is low, a speculator might come in and buy up a lot of shares cheaply. Speculators do this if they think the company will recover, or if they can buy enough shares to influence its direction and make it profitable once more.

All blag and bluster

Share prices are affected not just by announcements of profit and loss, but by other factors. A pharmaceutical manufacturer's shares will rise in value if it announces a new medicine to combat a common disease, for example. But if a medicine is withdrawn because of a safety scare, the share price will fall. It might also fall if a rival company launches a more successful product. The fall might occur even before the new product reaches the market – it's all a case of confidence and expectations. This is one reason why businesses put so much effort into maintaining a successful public image.

Sometimes a company can be brought down by its poor performance on the stock exchange even though it appears to be operating normally on a day-to-day basis. If its share value falls too far, banks will not allow an overdraft or loan, suppliers will not allow credit, and customers may fear that orders will not be fulfilled.

Shareholders risk their capital (in the form of invested money) in the hope of a good return. The dividends they are paid and the increase in the value of their shares is their reward for the risk they take – the risk of losing their money. It is not the same as the reward that workers receive, which is payment in return for their labour. To the worker, return on capital can look like money for nothing. A shareholder who holds stock for a matter of weeks, days or even hours and sells it again to make a quick profit, may earn more money than a worker makes in a whole year.

Successful traders in shares have a talent for speculating, or anticipating which shares will do well, and then buying and selling them at optimum moments. They have put time into learning about the stock market, but are not adding anything to the value of the firm's products. Whether a company's share price goes up or down a little makes scant difference to the performance of its products in the marketplace. But a significant change in share price can make a difference to market performance, often without reflecting any genuine change in the value of the products.

BULLS AND BEARS

When times are good, GDP is high and the economy is productive, economists speak of a bull market. In times of recession, unemployment, falling GDP and falling share prices, economists speak of a bear market. By the same token, an individual can be 'bullish' (optimistic and willing to invest) or 'bearish' (pessimistic and unwilling to invest).

The changing nature of speculation

Until the 1960s, most investors bought stock to receive dividends rather than to make a profit trading. Then people began speculating – buying and selling stock to make gains on the capital itself. The argument ran that this was not really speculating, as the true value of stock is whatever you can sell it for. Financial institutions then began offering more and more varied – and increasingly obscure – financial products to investors.

The standard financial product is the derivative, a product whose value is based on (derived from) the value of the underlying asset. During the 1990s, financial products multiplied, bearing less and less relation to the real businesses at the base of the structure. The 'products' being traded were often far removed from the productive asset – the share in a hotel, publishing company or other business that sold a genuine service or good.

Financial products proliferated to the point at which they could no longer be supported by the asset they were based on. By 2007, world GDP was $65.6 trillion (£42.5 trillion), but the value of the financial asset market was $900 trillion (£583 trillion). The financial sector was now largely independent of the industries on which it had been built.

Speculation pushes up the price of real goods and services. The World Bank estimated that, in 2010, 44 million people worldwide were pushed into poverty because of high food prices caused, in part, by speculators pushing up the price of basic commodities.

The growing parasite

Financial markets have filled with increasingly abstruse 'products' which have no bearing on real goods and services. They include buying and selling 'futures' (the promise to purchase goods at a fixed price at a future date) and reselling bundled insurance risks. Some economists, even previous financiers, are calling the financial industry 'parasitic'.

CHAPTER 22

Does aid help or hinder?

Overseas aid is a
contentious issue.

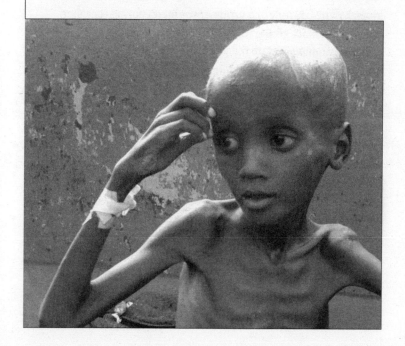

Some people question whether we should give aid to foreign countries at all when there are people at home in need. Then there is the broader question of whether aid actually has any impact or might even make the situation worse for people in developing countries.

Setting goals

The target set by the United Nations for developed countries is for each of them to spend 0.7 per cent of gross national income (GNI) on official development assistance (ODA) to less economically developed countries. In 2014, Denmark, Norway, Luxembourg and Sweden exceeded that target and the UK was on target. All other developed countries fell below it.

First and other aids

Aid can be allocated for short-term or long-term goals, it can be given by one country or a group of countries acting together, or by individuals giving to charity. It can be given with or without conditions.

Emergency aid is given to alleviate the immediate effects of a sudden disaster, such as earthquake, flood or famine, through rescue work and emergency food, shelter and medication. It is often supplied by charitable giving, including donations made by individuals, and handled by international aid agencies such as the International Red Cross and Medecins Sans Frontieres. Many national governments contribute to emergency aid financially and by providing food, medicines, equipment and specialist (often military) personnel.

Long-term development aid is given to raise standards of living in a country over time. It can follow on from emergency relief or be used to help a country that has been impoverished by long-term environmental, social or political problems. It aims to improve education, healthcare, infrastructure and other fundamental services so that people and economies can become more productive in the long term.

One country giving to another is called unilateral aid. An international organization such as the United Nations giving to a country is called multilateral aid. The aid might be financial or given in the form of supplies or expertise.

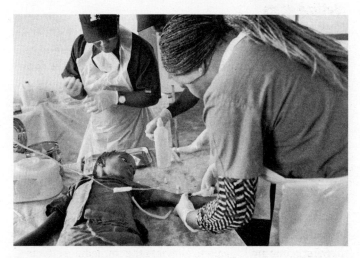

With and without strings

Aid given freely is called grant aid. More often, aid is tied or conditional, meaning it comes with strings attached. For example, it might be funding for a development (such as a dam or railroad), given on condition that the contract to build it goes to a business based in the donor country. The recipient benefits from the infrastructure (the new dam or railway) and the donor country benefits through increased employment and tax revenue from the participating company. The project usually employs local labour and may source materials locally, thereby injecting extra cash into the local economy.

This form of aid can benefit communities in the short term, through increased local employment and trading opportunities, and in the long term, by improving infrastructure. But it needs to be managed carefully or it can unbalance the local economy, pushing up prices and even leading to shortages. The requirement to use a contractor based in the donor country restricts choice in terms of pricing and the way in which the building work is carried out.

What is aid for?

The overall aim of aid is to raise living standards for the poorest people in the world, and to do it in ways that are sustainable. It is not just a matter of giving food to hungry people or tents to people whose homes have been destroyed in a hurricane (emergency relief); it involves helping to build fair economies in which no one is destitute and the community as a whole is economically productive. It's a tall order. The world's poorest communities struggle with some seemingly insuperable problems, including low-grade land, hostile climate, scant natural resources, political turmoil, oppression and war. These are not easy conditions in which to build a thriving economy.

There's no magic wand for transforming a poor economy into a healthy one. But there are many long-term measures that can provide a community with a more hopeful future, including the funding of education, vaccination programmes, healthcare, and essential infrastructure such as roads and a clean water supply. Funding (or loan of expertise) for these developments might not alleviate short-term needs, but it should build better prospects for the future. But economists' opinion on the effectiveness of aid is still divided.

Why give money away?

Support for foreign aid is far from universal. Many people argue they would rather have the money they pay in taxes used in their own country, for the benefit of the home population. But there are sound economic and political reasons for helping the poor in developing countries.

If it works, long-term development aid should make the world better for all of us. Oxford economist Paul Collier says that aid should be prompted first by compassion and second by 'enlightened self-interest'. The compassion we feel for less fortunate people prompts us to act, and enlightened self-interest keeps us motivated once we get into the nitty-gritty

THE MILLENNIUM VILLAGES PROJECT

An economist called Jeffrey Sachs at the Earth Institute, Columbia University, USA, started the Millennium Villages Project to provide a sustainable aid programme to villages in Africa. It aids the development of education, healthcare, sustainable local industries and sustainable agriculture. People are helped to start businesses and build homes and latrines, and there is an emphasis on training for the long term so that the changes endure and perpetuate.

There is a budget of $110 (£71) per villager per year for five years. This usually provides fertilizer and high-yield seeds, clean water, basic healthcare and education, mosquito bed nets, and a communications link to the outside world. Villages included in the scheme have seen increased agricultural productivity of up to 350 per cent. Sachs also promotes what he calls 'clinical economics', whereby a community's needs are diagnosed so that an individually targeted aid programme can be developed. Sachs has advised on aid to Russia, Poland and Bolivia – countries with very different needs.

of developing an aid programme. For example, enlightened self-interest may manifest in recognizing that there will be fewer economic migrants if people can find work in their own country, or that a developing economy will later become a valuable customer base.

Global productivity

When each country puts its resources to the best possible use, the whole world benefits and global productivity is increased. If the poor are desperate and without hope, they are more likely to join extremist organizations and support oppressive dictators who can destabilize a region through military conflict. Some may farm poppies for the opium trade or become refugees, asylum seekers and economic migrants. People who have a sustainable living in their own country tend to remain there.

Top down and bottom up

There are two broad approaches to aid: 'top down' and 'bottom up'. Top-down aid focuses on providing financial or other help to the government of a developing country in the hope that it will be distributed to the people most in need. This form of aid may come with restrictive conditions on how it should be used. Financial aid may be given in the form of a low-interest loan or debt relief (cancelling or reducing the interest on loans). Where aid is practical, in the form of equipment, food or the loan of expert staff, restrictions might be placed on exactly how it is to be used.

Bottom-up aid is largely administered by the donor and goes directly to the poorest people. One example is that of the International Red Cross distributing mosquito nets in Uganda. Because bottom-up aid does not work through the official distribution channels and networks within a country, it is often the only way of getting help to people in war-torn and disaster-struck areas where the transport infrastructure has been disrupted.

In general, larger sums are given as top-down aid, but there are more restrictions on its use.

WOMEN AT WORK

Studies by international aid agency Oxfam have found that one of the most effective ways to use aid in developing countries is to set up independent, female-run farm collectives. Here plots of land are farmed by women, and the produce is pooled and sold on the open market or through fair trade agreements. Money channelled through women in this way, rather than through the male community or tribal leaders, has led to improved crop yields, higher market prices and a marked improvement in the economic prosperity of the community – children, in particular.

Does it work?

Whether aid programmes work is a question debated by top economists. The following are a few of their criticisms:

- It is often stolen, misdirected or diverted from its intended destination and used to enrich the ruling elite and criminal gangs of the recipient countries.

- Instead of helping a community to develop a sustainable economy, it tends to engender a culture of dependency.
- It props up oppressive, undemocratic or corrupt regimes, preventing the society from adopting a fairer form of government.
- It can disrupt or destroy local markets by flooding the rural economy with cheap or free goods that make local produce uneconomic to produce and sell.
- It may be wrongly targeted or inappropriate – for example, food not recognized or unacceptable on dietary or social grounds may end up being wasted.

Making matters worse?

The American economist William Easterly has made many criticisms of top-down aid. In particular, he criticizes the effects of debt relief. Writing off debts, he suggests, does not release money for the poor but benefits the wealthy ruling elites who usually spend it abroad, in economically developed countries, without creating a trickle-down effect (see Chapter 9). He argues, too, that debt relief encourages overspending (in order for a country to secure the relief) and may result in further borrowing if the rulers of recipient countries believe that future debts will be written off. It is also unfair to those countries who do pay back their loans.

THE WORLD BANK

The International Monetary Fund (IMF) and the World Bank were created at the Bretton Woods Conference in 1944. The purpose of the conference and the institutions founded there was to regulate international finances and recovery after World War II. The aim of the World Bank is to reduce poverty through the promotion of foreign investment and international trade.

Easterly also criticizes the aid culture that denies or minimizes the role of poor countries in helping themselves. He prefers an approach he calls 'free development', which puts the needs, rights and desires of people in a developing

AN OLD-SCHOOL APPROACH?

Some of the traditional types of aid activity, such as building schools, are currently under scrutiny. The root cause of a lack of education is not always the absence of school buildings; it can be because children are not attending existing schools, or because of poor-quality (or absent) teachers. One study found that spending 50 cents (32p) on treating children for intestinal parasites in Kenya increased school attendance more effectively than building new schools. This was because children infested with worms were too ill to attend school. It cost 25 times as much to build a school as to treat all the children in a community.

In Mexico, parents were paid a stipend if their children attended school. This measure increased attendance by 85 per cent as it compensated parents for the fact that their children were no longer earning money.

country first, with the emphasis on their own ability to help themselves out of poverty and solve their own problems.

Five billion to one (billion)

In the mid-20th century, around one billion of the world's population were reasonably well off, while five billion lived in poverty. The situation has reversed, with many previously very poor countries, including China and India, growing as economic powers. Now most of the world's population lives in relatively prosperous countries, with just one billion living in the worst conditions. For these people, though, standards of living have deteriorated during the past 40 years. This is often because bad governance, poor infrastructure, military conflict and civil unrest have made it harder to distribute aid to them.

Smart aid

While William Easterly has voiced reservations about top-down aid and Jeffrey Sachs, with his Millennium Villages Project, supports intensive intervention, Esther DuFlo, Professor of Economics at MIT, advocates a middle approach. She recommends using 'smart aid' to evaluate and target aid interventions carefully. Citing ideology, ignorance and inertia as the main reasons for the failure of aid, DuFlo's approach is to carry out randomized, controlled trials of aid initiatives such as the distribution of bed nets to protect people from mosquitoes and the provision of education subsidies. The trials should reveal which interventions work and which don't, so that aid budgets can be used to the best effect.

> 'We have enough on the planet to make sure, easily, that people aren't dying of their poverty. That's the basic truth.'
>
> Jeffrey Sachs, director, Earth Institute, Columbia University

CHAPTER 23

How do we benefit from international trade?

Improved transport and the internet have made global trading easier than ever.

It can be difficult to tell whether it's best to buy goods produced in your own country or to embrace the world market. It seems that buying home-produced goods is good for our national economy, but it's not quite that straightforward. International trade has grown for a reason, and it can help to maximize world productivity.

Free trade and not-so-free trade

The two approaches to international trade are free trade and protectionist policy. Trade between countries without restrictions, tariffs or barriers, is known as free trade. The opposite, which tries to protect home production by banning imports or subjecting them to higher taxes or restricting them with a quota system, is a protectionist policy. There are advantages and disadvantages to both.

If one country is good at producing something cheaply, free trade means it can flood other markets and stifle local production. This is good for consumers, who can buy the item more cheaply, but it is bad for local producers, who might be forced out of business. In a protectionist market, producers don't have to try so hard; they can sell poor quality goods at high prices. The lack of competition means that consumers have no access to better and/or cheaper alternatives.

Trade and choice

One obvious advantage of international trade is that it gives consumers more choice. No country has the resources and conditions necessary to provide every possible product. Trade allows us to buy fruit and vegetables which don't grow in our climate and to make things with metals not mined from our own land. Without international trade, Scandinavian consumers could never enjoy mangos, no one in Britain could drink tea and Americans could not wear silk scarves.

Who's good at what?

When people moved from subsistence living (producing everything for their own households) to mercantile economies where they took on specialized jobs, the division of labour resulted in increased productivity. There are good reasons for encouraging specialization in the world market, too.

Let's say one country (Italy, for example) is good at producing olives and the other (Afghanistan, say) is good at producing goats. Imagine, for the sake of argument, that there are perfect trading conditions, and that neither Italy nor Afghanistan is putting its resources into any other kind of production. There are no transportation or storage costs to complicate the issue, and there is a good market for olives and goats in both countries.

Italy and Afghanistan each try to satisfy the home market for goats and olives. Their production is:

	Olives (million tonnes)	Goats (millions)
Italy	400	100
Afghanistan	200	300
Total	**600**	**400**

If Italy, which is especially good at producing olives, gave up goat-farming and concentrated on growing olives, it could increase production. Similarly, if Afghanistan gave up trying to grow olives and focused on goats, it would enjoy a veritable glut of goats.

	Olives (million tonnes)	Goats (millions)
Italy	800	0
Afghanistan	0	550
Total	**800**	**550**

(These figures are fictional – please don't sell your goat/olive farm on the basis of their projected rewards!)

Overall, the production of goats and olives has increased as in each country farmers are focusing on what they are good at and what their land is best suited to. Their farming is more efficient and more productive. In Italy, olive farmers have an advantage – an absolute advantage, as they are better at it – and in Afghanistan goat farmers have an absolute advantage because of their expertise. The two countries can trade, sharing the benefits of the improved production. The inhabitants of both Italy and Afghanistan can enjoy more olives and goats and, if there are too many, may even trade some with another country which is good at producing something different.

Who's not too bad at what?

But what if one country is better than its trading partner at producing everything? Let's take two more countries, Bolivia and Brazil. Each produces only coffee and cocoa; let's assume that Brazil is better than Bolivia at both.

	Coffee (million tonnes)	Cocoa (million tonnes)
Brazil	800	400
Bolivia	100	300
Total	**900**	**700**

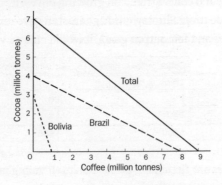

We can show the potential for each country to produce cocoa and coffee using a production possibility frontier curve (see below). Points A, B and C show how Brazil could split its resources between the two products.

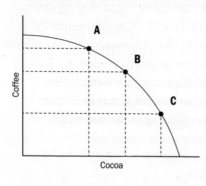

Brazil could produce lots more coffee, but only if it produced no cocoa, so it has an opportunity cost in cocoa. Brazil is twice as good at producing coffee as producing cocoa; it would have to give up two tonnes of coffee to produce an extra tonne of cocoa. Brazil has a comparative advantage in producing coffee. If we assume that the profit per tonne is the same for coffee and cocoa, Brazil would do much better to focus production on coffee, which it can produce more efficiently. Then it could trade with Bolivia to get cocoa. Bolivia has a comparative advantage at producing cocoa. Although cocoa production is not as efficient in Bolivia as in Brazil, it is less *inefficient*. Bolivia is *least bad* at producing cocoa, so should focus on that.

If Brazil gave up producing cocoa and Bolivia gave up producing coffee, their output would look like this:

	Coffee (million tonnes)	Cocoa (million tonnes)
Brazil	1600	0
Bolivia	0	600
Total	**1600**	**600**

This is good news for coffee drinkers, but a bad outcome for chocolate lovers as there is now less cocoa and much more coffee than previously. The best solution would be for Bolivia to give up producing coffee, but for Brazil to produce a small amount of cocoa to make sure the supply is sufficient to meet demand. The final production would look like this:

	Coffee (million tonnes)	Cocoa (million tonnes)
Brazil	1400	100
Bolivia	0	600
Total	**1400**	**700**

If a 'buy Bolivian' campaign encouraged people in Bolivia to demand Bolivian coffee, the economic situation in that country would be worse, not better, as farmers would have to grow the crop they were least good at producing.

At what price?

In order to trade, the two countries need to fix a rate at which coffee and cocoa (or olives and goats) will be exchanged. Clearly neither country wants to pay as much for the goods as it costs to produce them at home; if it did, there would be no point in trading. In Brazil, one tonne of coffee is 'worth' half a tonne of cocoa (opportunity cost), which can be written as:

$$1Cof = \frac{1}{2}Coc$$

As Bolivia produces three tonnes of cocoa for every tonne of coffee, the equivalent expression is:

$$1Cof = 3Coc$$

The two countries want to set terms which mean each is better off than it would have been just paying the opportunity cost to get the coffee/cocoa it wanted. They need to fix an exchange rate somewhere between a half and three tonnes of coffee for each tonne of cocoa. In this case, 1Cof = 1Coc sees both countries better off, but Bolivia benefits more. They might settle on:

$$1Cof = 1\tfrac{3}{4}Coc$$

because this is the midpoint between ½ and 3.

Global competition

For a country to be competitive globally, it must have a comparative advantage in several markets so that it can find trading partners. Natural resources give a country an advantage: Kuwait has oil reserves, Sicily has a climate suitable for growing lemons, and Iceland is surrounded by fish-rich seas. A country can give itself a competitive advantage through developing its human resources or by investing in a market it wants to build. In terms of international trade, it's best if the market being built is exportable. For example, Iceland wouldn't increase its international competitive edge by perfecting sledges, which are not wanted in many other places.

That's not all

Inevitably there are other factors that determine whether a country will trade successfully in world markets. Sometimes a country's lack of competitiveness is price-related:

- Exchange rate: if one country has a strong currency and the other country has a weak one, it will be difficult for the former to persuade the latter to pay enough for its goods to make trade profitable. A strong pound/dollar/euro is bad for exports.
- Inflation rate: if inflation is higher in one country than another, its exports will effectively rise in price in the importing country.

- Unit labour costs: if the cost in labour of producing each item goes up, the cost to the exporter will increase, and the item will be more expensive to the importer.

Other reasons for a country's lack of competitiveness include:

- Quality of product: if a country produces low-quality goods, these will be difficult to sell in a competitive market.
- Quality of service: good after-sales service and prompt delivery build a reputation that attracts further business, while poor service will lose business.
- Marketing: researching a market, making a product that meets customer requirements and advertising the finished product are important ways of creating enthusiasm in a market.
- Income elasticity: this is the change in wealth of customers in an economy. If people in a country have the money and motivation to spend on imports, exporters will be more successful in that market.
- Nationalism: people may prefer to buy home-produced goods. They may also prefer them because of a concern for the environment and a desire to minimize their carbon footprint.

Trade barriers

Governments sometimes introduce barriers to free international trade because they want to protect home producers. They do this through the introduction of tariffs (taxes on imported goods) and imposition of quotas, which limit the quantity of certain goods that can be imported. However, there are generally more losers than winners under a protectionist policy.

The winners are the domestic producers who are able to capture the home market. Their goods might be more expensive or of lower quality than the imports, but they will still be successful if they are all that is available to consumers. The losers are the consumers and the countries/businesses trying to sell goods as imports. Consumers will either have to pay more or to go without – especially if the home producers can't make enough to satisfy demand.

Protectionism is a strategy likely to backfire. Countries unable to sell their goods into the trade-restricted economy are likely to retaliate with tariffs or quotas of their own, damaging the protectionist country's ability to sell its exports. The only winners are the producers of goods in the home economy (and the government, as it collects revenue from the tariffs).

Besides tariffs and quotas, governments can pay subsidies to a home industry to help it compete. Governments can also introduce extra legislation, such as requirements for testing, making exporting into the country expensive and difficult.

Agreeing to it

A voluntary export restraint (VER) is like a quota, except that both countries agree to the restriction. It might seem odd that a country would agree to a restriction on its exports, but it can confer a financial advantage. If the supply of a product is restricted so there is not enough of it to meet demand, the price rises. So although the exporter can sell fewer units into the market, the price of each is higher. Japan and the USA had a VER which limited the quantity of Japanese cars imported into the USA between 1981 and 1994. The quota was agreed because cheap, fuel-efficient Japanese vehicles were threatening the US car industry. Japanese companies began to export larger, luxury vehicles to make the most profit possible from the restricted number of sales.

Free trade or not?

Most economists believe that free international trade is the better option. It should lead, through the principle of comparative advantage, to the most efficient use of world resources. But some countries want to impose trade restrictions to give infant (newly started) industries time to grow before having to compete in the harsh open market. This introduces its own problems: when should support be withdrawn? What if the infant market is ill-conceived and the country really has no comparative advantage in that area?

Another argument in favour of restriction is to prevent the aggressive dumping of cheap goods into one country's market in order to undercut domestic competition. The World Trade Organization, which polices free trade, makes provision for countries to combat this.

A slightly more compelling argument is that it is perilous for a country to be entirely dependent on other economies for key commodities. If a country has no domestic supply of food, fuel and essential raw materials, it could be held to ransom by other nations or left high and dry in the event of a war. The EU spends a lot of its budget shoring up the prices paid to European farmers through the Common Agricultural Policy; it does this to prevent the food markets being entirely dominated by cheap food from outside Europe (see Chapter 16). In an ideal world, we could assume that our trading allies would always be there with their supply of grain, gas, steel and so on – but we don't live in an ideal world.

Perhaps the most compelling argument against free trade, however, is made by Oxfam, Consumers International and Friends of the Earth. These charities point out that while there is an overall gain to the world economy, it all goes to a few huge multinational business organizations. The losers are developing nations, most consumers, and the environment.

CHAPTER 24

How do multinationals escape paying tax?

Evading tax is a crime, but avoiding it is not. And globalization makes tax avoidance easy.

In 2012, some major international corporations – including Google, Starbucks and Amazon – faced public outrage when it emerged that they were all paying very little or no tax in some of the countries in which they were operating.

In trouble with consumers

The companies in question were clearly doing a lot of business, but claimed they were not making a profit so should not have to pay corporation tax. Starbucks declared it had been making a loss in the UK for years – while telling its investors it was happy with the profitable UK arm of the company. The outcry led to boycotts. Amazon brazened it out; but Google is quite hard to boycott because it is everywhere.

Easy to boycott, Starbucks was the only company to throw a bone to its critics. In an attempt to silence its protestors, Starbucks agreed to pay £20 million ($31m) to the UK tax authorities, HM Revenue and Customs, despite maintaining it had done nothing wrong. This £20 million ($31m) was a drop in the ocean – Starbucks had paid only £8.6 million ($13.25m) in corporation tax between opening up in the UK in 1998 and 2012, despite making £3 billion ($4.6bn) in sales. It reported an operating loss every year and claimed that the company would not be making a profit until 2017.

Most of us would ask why, if a company has 500 coffee shops, does it make no profit? Or, if it has 500 coffee shops and makes no profit, perhaps it's not very good at the coffee business. Clearly Starbucks is pretty good at the coffee business and was not breaking the law. So how did they do it?

That'll be $4,000 (or £2,600) . . .

An international corporation is able to organize its business in such a way that, on paper, it makes most of its money in territories that impose the lowest rate of tax on profit. This may be a legitimate country, such as Belgium, or a tax haven, such as the Cayman Islands, which does very little other than hide money for people.

Let's assume that an imaginary business called Quickbuck has set up a chain of shops across Europe. Some European countries have much lower rates of corporation tax than others. In the UK, the corporation tax rate in 2012 was 24 per cent; in the Republic of Ireland (Eire), it was 12.5 per cent. It's obviously to Quickbuck's advantage to make its profit in Ireland rather than in the UK. But Ireland is tiny, smaller than most other European countries, so even if Quickbuck opened lots of shops there, it wouldn't be able to make most of its European profit in Eire. So it employs a nifty trick called transfer pricing. This involves selling or licensing goods to itself, from the tax haven country, for a hugely inflated price.

To do this, Quickbuck registers its logo in Eire and makes all its associated companies in other European countries license the logo at a hugely inflated price. Then Quickbuck insists that all its shops in Europe use (for example) a particular type of pricing gun, which it sells to each shop at £10,000 a piece, even though the gun could be bought for £50 from a local supplier. So the genuine profit of the other European stores is gradually eroded, squandered at the Irish headquarters of Quickbuck, where it will be taxed at only 12.5 per cent.

Bad or not?
What Quickbuck is doing is not illegal because the other European countries haven't regulated against it. They could do: some nations, including Japan, have in the past had quite stringent regulations to prevent transfer pricing. So Quickbuck is doing nothing wrong?

The argument for saying it is wrong is that Quickbuck is benefiting from goods and services put in place using taxpayers' money but is not contributing to these in any way. For example, Quickbuck is costing the taxpayer money by damaging the roads with its large lorries, but making no contribution to repairing the national infrastructure. Quickbuck may argue that it's providing employment and contributing to GDP. But all businesses are doing that, and they're contributing to the infrastructure as well. Quickbuck can be more competitive because its tax bill is lower. It can draw trade away from companies who are paying their fair share. Is that good business sense or the unethical exploitation of a loophole – or both?

Big losses

It might sound like a relatively infrequent problem, but it's not. An estimated $200 billion (£130bn) a year is lost to governments of developing countries through businesses using tax havens, in a practice known as 'profit laundering'. (Another $250 billion (£162bn) is lost through individuals using tax havens, including for criminal activity.) The total loss to world economies is $1 trillion (£648bn). As the entire global aid budget is less than $100 billion (£65bn), it's clearly a significant sum. No aid would be needed if the tax-haven loopholes were closed. Ironically for the UK, 35 of the 72 tax havens are British dependencies, territories or Commonwealth members, yet the UK is one of the big losers in profit laundering.

Doing business with yourself

There are other tactics that Quickbuck can use to reduce its tax liability. It can sell goods to itself at very low prices then move them into an area where there is low corporation tax, and herefore no disadvantage to making a profit. It can lend money to itself in different countries, charging itself a huge rate of interest as a way of moving money into a low-tax jurisdiction.

The UK government believes that 50–60 per cent of all world trade is between subsidiaries within the same umbrella company. This gives plenty of scope for profit laundering. Among the examples of pricing designed to take advantage of different tax rates are TV antennae sold out of China at US$0.04 (£0.025) and American bulldozers at $528 (£342). Overpriced items include German hacksaw blades, at $5,485 each (£3,556), and Japanese tweezers at $4,896 (£3,174).

Fairness triumphs

Despite all this, consumer pressure and government intervention have made a difference and multinationals are being called to account. In 2012, the UK government investigated and interrogated Amazon, Starbucks and Google and lambasted them for being 'unjust', 'immoral' and spouting 'unacceptable nonsense' in testimonies to the Public Accounts Committee. The EU's Taxation Commissioner has proposed closing the loophole that allows large multinationals to use 'aggressive tax planning'. In advance of changes in legislation, the prime targets of public criticism have begun to pay more tax in the countries where they operate. The US tax authorities have asked Amazon for a back payment of $1.5 billion (£970m).

PICTURE CREDITS